BETHAN RYDER

NEW RESTAURANT DESIGN

LAURENCE KING PUBLISHING

LAURENCE KING

Published in 2007
by Laurence King Publishing Ltd
361–373 City Road
London EC1V 1LR
T +44 (0)20 7841 6900
F +44 (0)20 7841 6910
E enquiries@laurenceking.co.uk
W www.laurenceking.co.uk

Text © Bethan Ryder 2007
This book was produced by Laurence King Publishing Ltd

A catalogue record for this book is available
from the British Library.

ISBN-10: 1-85669-500-X
ISBN-13: 978-1-85669-500-8

Designed by Richer Design

Printed in China

CONTENTS

The predecessor to this book, *Restaurant Design* (2004), briefly documented the history of public eating from antiquity to the twenty-first century, declaring that eating out had become as much a lifestyle choice and form of entertainment as a source of nourishment. The introduction concluded: 'Today restaurants can look like anything from a bedroom to a spaceship, from a Buddhist temple to a souk. Providing there is somewhere to rest a plate, when it comes to inspiration the world is the restaurant designer's oyster.'

Barely three years on, there is no abatement in the hunger for elegant, unusual and spectacular dining spaces. Indeed, an article in *Time* entitled 'Feast Your Eyes' (14 September 2004) observed: 'Atmosphere, cachet, sex appeal, status – all those are on the menu too, and it's largely the job of the décor to provide them. (Or to lure the crowd that completes the picture.) This is why restaurants are second only to museums as the places where designers get to take their audacious ideas out to play. In London and Milan, along the Pacific Rim, in Miami, Los Angeles and Bombay, restaurants are the hot design laboratories.' *New Restaurant Design* continues the story, profiling a further 46 restaurants from around the world completed between 2003 and 2006. These are presented into loosely defined thematic categories of design style: Global Views, New Baroque, Modern Classic and High Concept. These are not rigid definitions – some restaurant projects could fall into more than one category – but merely an attempt to capture some of the current key trends.

Since 2003 there has been a waning of the retro-futuristic style that merited an entire chapter called Retro-Pop. Something of a *fin-de-siècle* trend, it aimed to recreate the pop optimism of the 1960s and 1970s and was often influenced by films such as Kubrick's *2001: A Space Odyssey* (1968), combining contemporary hi-tech materials with furniture by designers such as Eero Aarnio and Verner Panton. David Rockwell Group's Pod in Philadelphia exemplified this trend. Although there were not sufficient new projects to warrant an entire chapter devoted to this theme, there are several restaurants featured here that can considered clear descendents of this aesthetic: Semiramis in Athens, Lever House in New York and The Line in Singapore.

In the last few years there has been a noticeable increase in organic influences. Designers have always looked to nature for inspiration, but presumably as we grow more aware of the fragility of the planet, such references are likely to increase. Flora and fauna appear in restaurant projects in every chapter; for example in murals of natural

LEFT
The Mies van der Rohe and Philip Johnson-designed Pool Room dining room at The Four Seasons restaurant (1959) in the Seagram Tower, New York. The mid-century modern classic is revered as one of the best examples of restaurant design by many of today's top designers.

BOTTOM LEFT
An example of Japanese-themed design in the main dining room at Megu, New York, by Glamorous (2004).

BOTTOM RIGHT
Pod in Philadelphia, by David Rockwell Group (2002), is the perfect example of the millennial trend for retro-futuristic interiors.

RIGHT
East Beach Café, Littlehampton, UK, Heatherwick Studio (2007). Heatherwick's unusual architecture reflects a continuing interest in organic forms.

scenery at Fin or butterfly motifs on the walls of Rama in Global Views. New Baroque features giant floral photo murals at Blits, mirrored pebbles at Gilt and silver tree sculptures at Cospaia. In Modern Classic natural influences include a courtyard garden at Moo, honeycomb forms at Lever House, and in its simplest form, acres of marble and richly veined timber at Fasano. In High Concept nature emerges in the trees of Restaurant 11 and Nobu Berkeley St, the organic, desert-like landscape of Fix, or the glass droplet chandeliers and the branch-like bar at Mix. Judging by schemes such as Thomas Heatherwick's East Beach Café in Littlehampton, on England's south coast – a structure which appears to be modelled from sand – our preoccupation with nature will continue to inspire innovative, outré forms, as well as providing two-dimensional artworks and decoration in commercial interiors.

GLOBAL VIEWS
Restaurants in this chapter feature designs inspired by, or incorporating aspects of, other cultures and countries, with Asia continuing to lead the way as a major influence in restaurant design in cities of the western world. Many interiors continue to be hybrids – often reflecting the cuisine on offer – as designers mix up their references in a post-modern way, borrowing what they fancy to create such pan-Asian venues as New York's Spice Market and Buddha-Bar. Other restaurants featured are examples of attempts at reinterpreting Japanese- or Chinese-themed interiors in a more subtle, contemporary way, such as Fin and Shibuya in Las Vegas, or Yauatcha in London. Although the trend for North African-influenced interiors seems to have waned, Dar El Yacout in Milan is a stunning example of a truly faithful representation of Islamic architecture and Moroccan design.

NEW BAROQUE
This style has really flourished over the last few years. As the venues in this chapter attest, exuberant lighting, decadence and pattern are all making a huge comeback – presumably to entertain, distract and seduce us in this age of anxiety. Many restaurants included here – such as The Mansion in Amsterdam, Gilt in New York and Le Cristal Room in Paris – fit the description New Baroque perfectly. Also included are projects that take their cues from this approach, yet are rather more contemporary, with just the odd extravagant flourish. Less about old-fashioned grandeur, these simpler interiors – such as Blits or Lágrimas Negras – are sprinkled with a few richly textured and patterned surfaces and materials. They are cleaner in their overall look but remain grandiose in spirit.

Many designers are using modern technology inventively to recreate old techniques or effects that are no longer feasible today, for example the 'lacework' walls of Isola Bar & Grill, the Sistine ceiling replicas at The Mansion, and the enormous, distressed reproductions of seventeenth-century paintings at Buddakan. Lately, it seems as if designers, like their fashion industry counterparts, are keen to explore the dark side, with a touch of the gothic creeping in. Bon Moscow and even Cospaia's dark dining room may well be signs of what is to come.

MODERN CLASSIC
The restaurants in this chapter are simple dining spaces that are often inspired by, or feature classic designs from, the twentieth century. These interiors don't tend to rely on any design tricks, themes or grand gestures. Instead, many designers rely on the beauty of natural materials – such as marble and stone – for adornment. Examples include Fasano in São Paulo, The Modern in New York and Canteen in London – all clearly influenced by mid-century modernism. Also included here are Lever House and The Line, which might have been categorized as retro-futuristic in the last book.

HIGH CONCEPT
This is a catch-all category for dining wonderlands where the designer has really let his or her imagination run wild. Many restaurants included here display design or technical innovations, such as Mix or Evo, while others are simply underpinned by a strong concept or vision, such as the all-black Black Calavados and the candy-coloured Semiramis. Many display organic forms and elements, such as Nobu Berkeley St, Restaurant 11, Fix and Senderens.

As for the future, many argue that design fatigue has set in, but you can bet that 'statement' restaurants will continue to open, particularly in cities such as Las Vegas, Dubai, New York and London, where public life is a parade, consumption is conspicuous and dining is a voyeuristic activity. In the following pages we feature 11 of the world's top restaurant designers and architects, who tell us about their ideal brief, how they work with clients, how they develop concepts, and where they like to eat out. Many, including the author herself, often prefer to frequent neighbourhood bistros, cafés and brasseries, but lavish, designer affairs will continue to dazzle, luring us in for the odd big night out. That is the great thing about restaurant design today – there really is something for everyone, every mood and every occasion. Long may it flourish.

Rob Wagemans – Concrete Architectural
Associates
(Supperclub, Nomads, Blender, Envy, Mansion,
Morlang, Local...)

We like clients with passion, who understand why they're
doing what they're doing, but who also have an open
mind. Our approach is logical and simple: we don't
overcomplicate design. The process involves finding the
essence of the issue – dependent on what kind of customer
the client is seeking to attract, the type of food, or the
market demand – through a series of discussions. We meet
in the client's office and in our office, because people react
differently in a different environment, and we always go to
dinner too, because that's really sociable. You get a better
understanding of the client and they have the guts to tell you
what they do, or don't, want – which is often more
illuminating.

We steer clear of projects overseen by a financial director or
by managers, because often such people are too insecure
about their own jobs to create something new. We have
difficulties with people who can live with concessions,
because it's not possible to create something that everyone
likes – this does not exist – so you just become very generic
and we like to make specific things. Take the Supperclubs in
Amsterdam and Rome – they are restaurants a lot of people
love, but there are others who say, 'there's nothing there for
me' and that's good. If you're specific, then you create
something that generates discussion and stops the world
being boring, and makes it a little bit more beautiful instead.

Really good restaurants are about honesty in design, but
they are also about food. Every good business has a
certain kind of passion and an emotional level to it, and not
too much rationale. In the best restaurants the chef is often
the owner and he cooks with his heart. Such a client wants
an interior that does the same thing and if you have
harmony between the kitchen staff and the restaurant, the
logo, the look and feel, and the patrons, it works really well.

My ultimate restaurant project...

We are trying to be as multidisciplinary as possible, so my
dream is to create architecture, interior design, product
design and graphic design that are all in harmony. So my
ultimate project would be anything where we can design
the entire package.

I wish I'd designed...

The Four Seasons in New York (see page 4). It opened in
1959 but is still one of the most beautiful restaurants in the
world and people flock there every night and enjoy it as a
special place. That's brilliant.

My favourite three restaurants are...

MACARONI, Rome. A very small Italian restaurant where if
you ask for pasta with truffle you get simply pasta, cream
and truffle, but it tastes fantastic.
GEORGES, the Centre Pompidou, Paris. For the food
quality, the location and the brilliant mixture of cultural life
and culinary life – as a museum restaurant it's a pioneer.
ENVY, Amsterdam. You can always pop in, it's about good
food and wine, the people are nice and it's simple, you
don't have to wear your Gucci shoes.

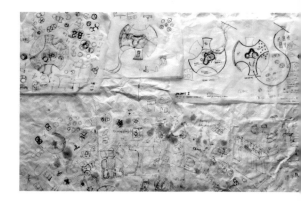

FAR LEFT
Le Bed Baroque, the communal
dining chamber at Supperclub
Roma, Rome, Italy, Concrete
Architectural Associates (2002).

TOP LEFT
Rob Wagemans, Concrete's founder.

TOP CENTRE
Dining in silver clouds on the rooftop
of the Centre Pompidou, at Georges,
Paris, France, Jakob + MacFarlane
(2000).

TOP RIGHT
Simplicity rules at Envy, Amsterdam,
Concrete Architectural Associates
(2005).

ABOVE
Early concept sketches by the
Concrete crew for future restaurant
projects in Singapore.

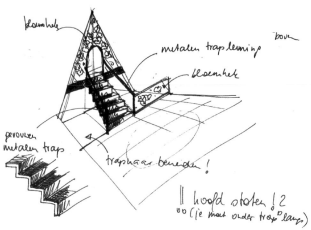

TOP LEFT
Marcel Wanders.

TOP RIGHT
Wanders designed an
intriguing shed-like
structure to house the
stairs leading down to
the restrooms at THOR,
The Hotel on Rivington,
New York (2004).

ABOVE
Sketch for the dining
salon at Blits, Rotterdam.

Marcel Wanders – Marcel Wanders Studio (Thor, Blits, Fifteen…)

I know something about hospitality, but not everything, so if I want to create a successful restaurant I only do it if someone is willing to work with me. I wouldn't even start if they don't have an idea about what they want to do. Discussion is always part of the design process – good clients know something about design and what they need, and then together we can create the best thing. Deciding whether to undertake a restaurant commission is really a question of the people; I need to feel respected and understood and I'm sure that the client wants the same thing. It also needs to be a challenge and a certain size, although that's not everything. The total volume of Blits wasn't huge but I knew the guys for some time, they were friends of mine. So it's those kind of things. What makes a successful restaurant is real hospitality, understanding who your customer is and giving them the best time ever, that's key. You recognize that in the food, the way the staff smile, the quality of the chairs, the tables, everything you see – that is what you want, to be taken care of in a beautiful way, a fun way; it all comes down to hospitality.

My ultimate restaurant project…

I would love to do a very small, secret restaurant in one of the canals of Amsterdam. It is underwater and no-one knows where it is, but people talk about it. It's small with ten tables or so, and the food is extraordinary.

My favourite three restaurants are…

LUTE RESTAURANT, Ouderkerk aan de Amstel
BON, Moscow, Philippe Starck
UNNAMED RESTAURANT, Amsterdam. The canals of Amsterdam form a complex structure of vaults and walls. The dark spaces inside this vast underground structure have had different functions in history: during the Second World War people found shelter here. Now a very exclusive restaurant is located below water level, entrance is by invitation only. We are not allowed to reveal the name or the exact location, but it's one of Marcel's favourites.

Adam D. Tihany – Tihany Design
(Le Cirque, Per Se, The Line, Aureole, Lafite…)

I like a client who knows who they are, not necessarily where they want to go or how to get there, but who have a strong sense of themselves, because I see myself as a portrait artist more than a restaurant designer. I like to get to know the person, a lot of chef clients don't have the necessary verbiage to describe in design terms what they want, but all of them can cook, so I ask them to cook a meal for me that they would serve at their restaurant and then I imagine the sort of establishment that would serve that food. Another metaphor for this might be giving them a custom-made suit… they feel really comfortable in it and they know it's specially made for them, tailored to their personality.

We start by carrying out a feasibility study; the client might ask for an open kitchen, or a certain number of seats, and then we see if we can fit in those requirements. We turn down more than we take on. I don't like to take on projects that don't have either a chef or a restaurateur who is very passionate. I'm not interested in a group of lawyers who just want to open a restaurant. I wouldn't want to do chain restaurants either and repeat something. We have a really small practice and I keep it small on purpose, so we have to be pretty selective. Also, I have to consider whether the next project will move us forward, we want to keep doing original things.

It's true to say that there are always opportunities for overkill with design, and in cities like New York, where people also pay a very high premium on design, sometimes the design overshadows the food experience, but there is space for everybody. There are people who value design more than they truly care about food, and that's fine. Why not? People pay very high premiums on the value of entertainment, they don't go out to eat because they're hungry, but because they want to have fun… why not! In cities like Las Vegas or Dubai the value that people place on entertainment is enormous – they go to forget their daily lives, they go to experience something else, to be in another world for a few hours, which is fine, but it's good when the food works because there are people who really care about the food.

There are three ingredients: food, service and design. A really successful restaurant has a great balance between all three. Very few achieve that kind of perfection, but that's the ultimate goal.

My ultimate restaurant project…
I would love to design one restaurant in every great city. Cities fascinate me and I'd love to work in many because then I'd get to spend time in them – Barcelona, Moscow, Beijing, Mumbai, Cairo, Marrakesh, Oslo…

I wish I'd designed…
The Four Seasons in New York (see page 4). It's a classic, it's a timepiece, something that happened at an important juncture in design, the stars were aligned, but there are lots of others too.

My favourite three restaurants are…
CHEZ ANDRÉ, Paris. It's on rue Marbeuf in the 8th arrondissement.
FRENCH LAUNDRY, Yountville, California. I loved it the first time I walked in there, it was on my honeymoon, it was everything.
GUNDEL, Budapest. I love this place. I designed it twelve years ago. It's like a beautiful turn-of-the-century restaurant.

ABOVE
Adam D. Tihany.

LEFT
Tihany designed all three incarnations of Le Cirque in New York for Sirio Maccioni. The latest, inspired by a circus 'big top', was completed in 2006.

CENTRE
Tihany adores chef Thomas Keller's historic-looking French Laundry, Yountville, California.

LEFT
Patrick Jouin.

BOTTOM LEFT
Concept sketch
by Patrick Jouin
on hotel
stationery.

Patrick Jouin
(Spoon St. Tropez, Chlösterli, Alain Ducasse at Plaza Athénée, Mix, Gilt…)

Mostly we work with an open brief. When we work with Alain Ducasse, he doesn't necessarily know what he wants, so it's an open brief in a sense, but he knows what will *not* work. It's about function and what the customer will experience when they are in the place, getting the mix right with the food and service, the light, the sound – he knows very well how a restaurant works, but he never discusses the decoration. After we've discussed the practicalities we will present our scheme and he reacts and says it is ok, or that this might not work for service reasons. It's always a rich, collaborative process. We say no to people who think we are just decorators, or who are without passion, or doing it just for business.

We start with the big picture; we examine the quality and weakness of each space. We practise interior architecture but always relate it to context and what is already there. It's hard to design brand new restaurants where there is a soul, you can't design history, you can't design time passing, but if there is at least a poetic intention it's always great. When it's just a copy or compilation of things seen in a magazine it's boring.

I don't know what the ingredients are for a successful restaurant, if I knew we would always be successful! It's not about budget, but the passion of everyone and the right combination of area, food, décor – the right balance is all.

My ultimate restaurant project…
To open a restaurant when it's not totally finished, just to say: okay it's nice now, let's stop. Like when you do a painting and just before the end you know it's better than when it's perfectly finished. Why? Because it's a dream. We try to create the most beautiful thing ever built in a particular time and it's always a failure. So, it's a good way to escape that and leave something that is unfinished. Maybe one day we will have a client who'll agree to let us do this.

I wish I'd designed…
I still love the Four Seasons in New York (see page 4) – it's the proportions and the small bar.

My three favourite restaurants are…
I GOLOSI, Paris. It's in my neighbourhood and I'm always there because I like the people. It's a very good Italian restaurant, you greet everyone with kisses and you spend half the time speaking with the chef – you feel part of the family.
PEASANT, New York. It's great, the guy cooks everything in a big wood oven and when you enter it smells so good.
AUX LYONNAIS, Paris. I like this small Alain Ducasse place.

RUA RODRIGO DA FONSECA 88 • 1099-039 LISBOA • PORTUGAL

Stephane Dupoux – Dupoux Design (Nikki Beach, Pearl, Cocoon, Touch Restaurant, Buddha Bar, Pre:Post…)

I love an open brief, I can't really work with clients telling me what do, although the lead might come from the client in terms of what the objective of the operation is and how you want to entertain your patrons: the food, the drinks, the cocktails. From this we create the layout, to ensure that people can move around and interact well. Circulation is the most important thing. A lot of people can choose colours, details and dress up a room, but getting the flow right is crucial.

We prefer to work with clients who are experienced in the hospitality market, because the success of a place is not only about design, or the food, it's about teamwork. A place is successful because the team is right. Design is important because it's what you see and feel – we are guided by our senses, every time we enter a space, there are reasons why you feel comfortable or uncomfortable, but once you've achieved that, then the food, the staff and the service have to be excellent to ensure a good experience. If it's all good you will come back. To make it successful for a long period of time it's about teamwork.

My ultimate restaurant project…

The first time they put a resort on the moon I'd like to be a part of it! I'd love to be able to put chairs and tables on the ceiling for once.

I wish I'd designed…

There are so many, but particularly Fleur de Lys in Las Vegas. It has a great chef, it's an amazing restaurant.

My favourite three restaurants…

CAFÉ DES ARTS, Cassis, France. Van Gogh on the wall, artists who paid in drawings, those places are full of energy and the food is amazing.
LA BASTIDE DE MOUSTIERS, Moustiers-Sainte-Marie, France. This Alain Ducasse restaurant is in a little medieval village perched on top of a mountain with a beautiful view of the valley below.
ZUMA, London.

TOP LEFT
Stephane Dupoux.

TOP CENTRE
Dupoux's design for Cocoon, London (2004), was inspired by a butterfly chrysalis.

TOP RIGHT
Pre:Post, New York, Dupoux Design (2006).

ABOVE
One of Dupoux's favourites, La Bastide de Moustiers, Moustiers-Sainte-Marie, France.

David Collins – David Collins Studio
(Locanda Locatelli, The Wolseley, J. Sheeky,
Petrus, Nobu Berkeley St...)

I prefer a brief that evolves around a personality, or the type of food on offer. This often helps to find the ideal building or location. A totally open brief can result in a restaurant that is neither one thing or another. It's difficult because I often think that some restaurants look too themed and too designed. A careful balance is essential and this comes from restaurant operators who know their customer and their price point and what they want to deliver. Often working within the existing building constraints is frustrating for architects and designers. Essentially, what the customers see is the restaurant, but what we have to contend with are the practical and functional difficulties, all the back-of-house aspects. With some buildings, by the time air-conditioning and proper services are installed ceiling heights can be really compromised. I've been quite inspired by trips to South America where land is less of a premium and people actually build new restaurants. That's something I would like to do more in the future.

I begin by thinking: what do I want to do? Do I like these people? Is it an interesting project? Then I probably put it out of my mind for a few days and think over things I've seen that could be useful or inspiring. I turn down most of the restaurant projects that we are asked to do. This is not just because I have become busy, or have a higher profile, so to speak, but because some people are completely unversed in what restaurants and looking after people entails. I have to like the people and feel that they are committed and passionate about it. There is no point in working with people if they are only half involved or if they are doing it as a vanity project or if, unfortunately, they're under financed – meaning that realistically what they want to achieve doesn't match their budget. If, on the other hand, it is a very small project, then you cut your cloth according to your measure. Sometimes it is about the money, but very often it's about whether it is interesting or I think it will work. I want to be involved with successful businesses.

My ultimate restaurant project...
I go to Milan quite often and, although I love the city, I find that the number of restaurants is quite limited, especially in view of what fabulous produce and cooks

they have there. Some of the designer restaurants are over-designed... and some of the old restaurants have had bad makeovers, so I would like to design a restaurant in Milan.

I wish I'd designed...
The Café de Flore and its neighbour Les Deux Magots, in Paris. They're chic, they're busy, they are beautifully lit and located in one of the most beautiful cities in the world, in one of the most beautiful locations in that particular city. Everything about them is right: understated and gorgeous.

My three favourite restaurants are...
EAT, Madison Avenue, New York. I am not a restaurant person, I am more of a café person. Whenever I am in New York I have breakfast here.
HOTEL COSTES, Paris. Because it combines camp, fashion, shallowness and sex in quite a funny and attractive way.
HOTEL FASANO, São Paulo (see pages 108–111). There are a number of restaurants in South America I love – many of them are on the beach, but a great favourite is this fabulous brasserie with amazing food.

Wolfram Putz – Graft
(Fix, Stack...)

We like to work with an open brief from a client who knows what that means and entails. I like clients who then know what they want when they've seen our suggestions, but in general – it is always a mix – a shared authorship with a positive attitude carries the farthest. We start with a team brainstorm the moment inspiration arises, whether that's a metaphor, a music piece, an association with nature, the taste of the food, the context – the spark will come when looking at it together.

We don't like to undertake projects that are not trying to do something new, that are trying to please a 'known' feeling, repeat a former success, or that is not interested in risking a bit of an innovative approach. The ingredients that make a successful restaurant are never the same, you always want to be surprised by the new ingredient, the unknown combination. Designing a restaurant is important – but the most important thing is always food and service...

My ultimate restaurant project?
Something in an extreme setting, where inside and outside can melt without walls, sitting in a large lake, in dry, half-submerged cosy areas, walls only barely above water level to keep the water out. Where your head is at water level and service comes via boat to you.

I wish I'd designed...
Always the unbuilt one, stuck in a drawer somewhere – we've got a couple of those.

My favourite three restaurants...
RESTAURANTS IN CLASSIC OLD EUROPEAN TRAINS – so you move while eating.
THE TABLE WITH CANDLES ON THE LONELY BEACH. The essence is the design of time on your table: used glasses, open bottles, dirty dishes rotating with the next course, an orchestra of experiences.
AN OLD JAPANESE INN from an unknown designer, where time has designed the patina of the experience.

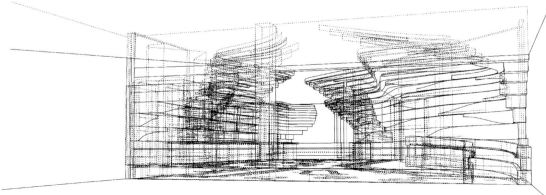

TOP LEFT
From left: Thomas Willemeit, Wolfram Putz and Lars Krückeberg of Graft.

CENTRE LEFT
Stack (2006) at the Mirage casino, Las Vegas, by Graft, was inspired by organic, canyon-like forms.

LEFT
Sketch for Stack showing Graft's distinctve internal architecture.

ABOVE
Bernard Khoury.

RIGHT
Drink below the
stars at the
rooftop bar of
Centrale, Beirut,
by Bernard
Khoury
Architects
(2001).

Bernard Khoury – DW5
(Yabani, Centrale, Aïshti, Black Box)

I'm truly incapable of working with an open brief; I think what makes an interesting project is its specificities. It's not really like we've reinvented a recipe or anything, but I see my work as an attempt to be as pertinent as possible in every given situation, which every time is very different. We try to avoid the obvious solution or answers. I'm very suspicious about architectural recipes, every scenario has its impossibilities and it's sometimes out of these that the non-obvious and the most interesting things come up. Sometimes they have nothing to do with the initial questions that are raised.

We refrain from drawing for a long time, we push it as late as possible, in fact I think the most interesting projects have been those when we did not allow pens or papers in our initial meetings, so instead we talked. Discussion liberates you from trying to spit something out on paper too early on in the process. I'm not saying drawing is not important, but I think it has its time and it comes much later in the process. Perhaps you can qualify this approach as more conceptual.

I couldn't work with stupid clients and I don't like cute restaurants or bars, I don't think they're the most interesting places. I don't go to these bars and restaurants. A place has to tell you something besides being cute and fashionable. What makes a place is so many things, designers are just part of the whole and I think we should embrace what makes a place and its context. By context I mean its social, economical, political and cultural context – sometimes things that are not so obvious. As for successful restaurants, the foremost important ingredient is the food.

My ultimate restaurant project…
It would have to do with its environment and environment is a very vast and broad term, you have to be turned on by the scenario you're presented with. Our part of the world [Lebanon] raises far more burning and dramatic questions which you're faced with and which you cannot avoid. The problems are so obvious, especially when it comes to entertainment, and the situations are very interesting. I like tough situations, and I don't like cute, happy little stories. That's not my department.

My favourite three restaurants are…
VARUJ, Beirut. It's a little Armenian restaurant in the Armenian quarter in Beirut. It's a great joint, fantastic, and they don't send you a bill, they just look at you and give you a price. If they like you it's very cheap.
CENTRALE, Beirut. I'm there very often, in the bar upstairs.
APO, Beirut. Another Armenian place, it's a disgusting little joint.

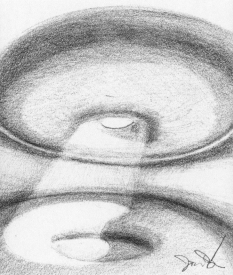

Jordan Mozer – Jordan Mozer Associates (Herzblut, Nectar, Canter's, East, Anna Mae/Mikado, Copper Bleu, Porthouse…)

My history professor in architecture school told me that Michelangelo did his best work when he had a very restricted brief, and we find that the more our clients know their businesses and are very clear about their aims then the easier it is to come up with a solution. When things are too open it is more difficult. We only turn restaurant projects down if the schedule is unrealistic or the clients are not so well-seasoned in their business, or if we're too busy.

The process begins with ensuring everything works in plan. We start with the relationship of the parts, try to address the functional aspects and building code requirements – that comes first. Only after those solutions are evident and clear, although still flexible and malleable, do we start to mess around with aesthetics. I use colour as a tool very early on to understand how the spaces relate to each other, and I also make three-dimensional sketches. We go from line sketches, little doodles, to perspective drawings, to watercolour paintings and also clay and cardboard models. It's a very organic process with many concurrent layers of study. We use the computer to manipulate the floor plan and get various vantage points. How much we use the

computer depends on the nature of the emotional content of the space; if we want a space that feels slick and machinelike, we'll do a computer rendering. If we want a place that feels rougher and sexier – a contrast between industrial and baroque perhaps – then it may be more appropriate to do watercolours. We really like imagining things from the big scale down to the tiniest detail, so it's a kind of magical realism where you walk in and we've created a consistent reality throughout.

In every restaurant there's a relationship between the food, the service and the environment. There are places where I'm very happy to go to that are ugly, with unpleasant lighting and great food, and they're inexpensive and I'm fine with that. Then there are other places, upscale casual environments that are designed to make you feel a certain way, excited, or peaceful, or luxurious, or calm, and the food contributes to that. So it's the whole package. I don't see it as a fight between the two but, as with any experience, it's a combination of all sorts of things.

The foundation of good restaurant design is creating a safe place that functions efficiently, within the pre-determined schedule and budget, but that's just the foundation. A great design has enormous emotional power: channelling the moment, embodying popular culture, visually expressing the culinary art that is being practised there, the personality of the host, the

soul of the neighbourhood and the fantasies of the guests.

My ultimate restaurant project…
Cities offer more opportunity to do sophisticated restaurants with a lot of idiosyncracy, the people are less conservative. So it would be creating a new building in a dense urban situation – New York, London, Shanghai, Moscow… That's attractive.

My favourite three restaurants are…
LA COUPOLE, Paris. The mythology of La Coupole has inspired thousands of imitators and millions of guests, and will continue to do so.
GENE & GEORGETTI STEAKHOUSE, Chicago. It's the prototypical Chicago steakhouse that dates back to 1941.
THE DINER IN THE MOVIE *DINER*. Like those first mid-century American diners that grew up with superhighways, composed from the materials and methods and impossible optimism and ideology of the transportation industry, a fantasy for a people rushing into the future with no time for the past.

Frank Tjepkema – Tjep.
(Fabbrica, Restaurant Praq...)

Usually the client has a particular direction and idea; the best thing is the dialogue and the collaborative process. It's often easier to be very creative in the context of boundaries than in a totally open situation. We begin by investigating a theme: if we're dealing with an Italian restaurant we investigate all the clichés and metaphors and try to break down those conventions. We also try to do something that is relevant for the area and not totally alien, for instance with Fabbrica we were dealing with an old warehouse in the industrial context of the harbour in Rotterdam and so we let ourselves be inspired by that. Food is obviously the most important aspect in a restaurant – if the food isn't good then people won't return, whereas if you have very good food but an ugly restaurant people might come back. Service and food are top priorities, and interiors are an absolute plus as a talking point, or for people to remember the place, or to get into certain moods. It's like a band – you need the drum and the bass but you can do without the trumpets. There are no rules that lead to the design of a great restaurant except one: a space gets a soul when it truly represents the enthusiasm and passion of the people who run it. If that's not the case, then it becomes artificial.

My ultimate restaurant project...
One where we design everything from the interior to the branding and identity. We prefer to work with small clients who give us a lot of freedom than with big corporations that might restrict us, but on the other hand, big corporations might have projects with a higher profile.... so they can be interesting from that perspective. We like to be able to explore new ideas.

My favourite three restaurants are...
SKETCH, London. It's the pod toilets. It's radical, funny and functional because the toilets mix men and women and they are a truly social space, that's very clever.
THE DELANO, Miami. The lobby and restaurant because it's a masterpiece of style and atmosphere. It's mysterious, spatial, poetic and dramatic at the same time!
PARADE'S THE BIG WHEEL. There's a Dutch touring circus called Parade which has a big wheel with seats for about 12 people. Every time your cabin passes the ground floor you can order food and it's served on the next rotation. My dream would be to create a permanent restaurant based on the same concept but ten stories high!

ABOVE
Tjepkema's sketch for a dining table at Restaurant Praq.

TOP RIGHT
Reflection of the space-age style toilet pods at Sketch, London (2003).

TOP LEFT
Frank Tjepkema and Janneke Hooymans of Tjep.

LEFT
The lobby restaurant at the Delano Hotel, Miami, Philippe Starck (1995).

FAR LEFT
George Yabu and Glenn Pushelberg.

LEFT
Blue Fin (2002), New York, Yabu Pushelberg.

RIGHT
Sketch for a future Yabu Pushelberg restaurant at the Mandarin Oriental hotel in Mumbai, India.

Glenn Pushelberg – Yabu Pushelberg
(Blue Fin, Fin, Maimon Wine & Grill, Shibuya, Simon LA…)

We prefer an intelligent client who has clarity to know what they want in terms of the direction, but there's still enough scope that allows you to explore and create something interesting – that's good. If you have a client who hasn't had experience of dealing with designers then the process is a little bit more challenging sometimes. We turn down projects that are more thematic or traditional in their approach, that's not really what we're good at.

We are contemporarists, but it doesn't necessarily have to be avant-garde or leading edge as long as there's a contemporary element to it… we're trying to create emotional experiences in restaurants. Other restaurant designers call them theatrical experiences and there's maybe a little bit of theatre involved, but for us successful restaurants deal with the patrons' emotions rather than theatre. It's a subtler approach, a lot of throwaway restaurant design kind of makes a theatre out of the whole experience and that results in an exaggeration of form, witty things that are one-line jokes. We're more interested in using the tools of interior design, whether its proportion of space, lighting, colour, materials, texture, or a sense of discovery, to create an emotional response to an interior. We like to determine what that should be. It's about creating a mood also based on what the context of the place is. All of those parts working together can create a restaurant that has a greater longevity to it. It's important to understand what the clichés are, and to steer away from them we aim to create a uniquely different language with each project.

As for what makes a successful restaurant, years ago someone asked us to make the ultimate Canadian restaurant. He had a great location on the top storey of a Mies van der Rohe tower in Toronto. So we got together with the chef, the maître d' and the manager, and we all wrote down a brief about what the ultimate Canadian restaurant would be in terms of service, food, and so on. Then over dinner we presented our briefs and from these we came up with an overall vision. That was an interesting exercise, to create a dining experience that holistically works from the food to the tabletops, service and type of environment. It created a brief that was not one person's perspective, it was a very smart way to work.

Our ultimate restaurant project…
It would be great to design an iconic place in Paris, because it's obviously one of the food capitals of the world, but other than the classic old restaurants I can't remember any beautiful modern restaurants. A refined restaurant in the food capital of the world would be a very interesting challenge.

Our favourite three restaurants…
LA ESQUINA, New York. A hidden gem that falls under the radar. We love the vibe, it's as if this was the way New York restaurants used to be before they became 'restaurants on steroids'. You enter the dining room from a downstairs entrance, which you have to walk through the kitchen to get to.
CAL PEP, Barcelona. The ultimate historic seafood-tapas bar in the old town of Barcelona with counter service, great waiters, authenticity – it's been around for ages and will never change. We love to visit it time and time again.
MUTSUKARI, Tokyo. The perfect modern Japanese restaurant. New and interesting, the cuisine is modern but its roots are based in authentic Japanese recipes. The atmosphere, service and food are just perfect.

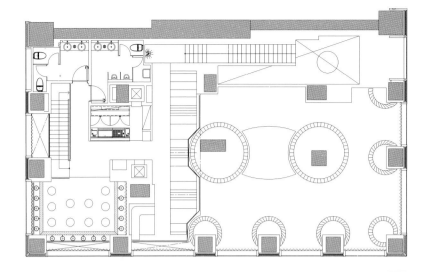

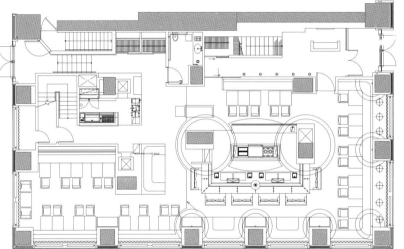

FAR LEFT
Megu's iconic
lampshades measure
around 3 metres (10 feet)
in diameter and are 4.8
metres (16 feet) high.

TOP LEFT
Plan of the 109 square
metre (1,170 square foot)
mezzanine level. The
giant shades mask
essential support
columns.

BOTTOM LEFT
Plan of the 273 square
metre (2,940 square
foot) ground-floor level.
The entire restaurant
accommodates 115
diners.

Hot on the heels of the success of Megu in TriBeCa, Yasumichi Morita and his Japanese-based team Glamorous returned to New York to design a second Megu in midtown Manhattan. It opened two years after the original, in April 2006. For the first, Megu owner Mr Koji Imai asked Morita to 'introduce real Japanese beauty to New Yorkers'. Glamorous responded by artfully blending Japanese artefacts into the interior – notable elements include a porcelain screen composed of sake bottles and rice dishes stacked atop each other, and the rich patchwork of exquisite antique kimono obi fabric that decorated the walls and ceiling of the Kimono Bar.

For the considerably smaller Megu Midtown, Imai asked only that the designers 'avoid the situation where the first is good but the second not so good, like a Hollywood sequel'. Rather than expressing Japanese beauty in an obvious way, Morita decided

the follow-up should be more 'sophisticated and evolved'. Ever ready to exploit the phototropic nature of humans, Glamorous design interiors that employ a dramatic interplay of light and shadow to theatrical effect. Megu Midtown is full of such contrasts.

The restaurant occupies the ground and mezzanine floors (kitchens are in the basement) of the Trump World Tower. The host building's huge structural columns, essential support for a tower block, posed the biggest challenge. Lighting wizard Morita's solution was to transform these obstacles into an iconic design feature: eight giant lampshades strung with wooden beads hand-carved in China. Clearly visible from the street, these mammoth shades radiate a warm glow, enticing patrons into the restaurant.

By contrast, the entrance is decidedly noir, with black granite floors, black timber panelled walls and a

bespoke black crystal Swarovski chandelier. Diners are guided to the mezzanine by an illuminated stairway, which features back-lit risers made of graphic sheets printed with a photograph of a waterfall and ukiyo-e images of carp.

The bar is similarly monochrome, moody and low-lit, with white travertine floors and predominantly black furniture, including granite-topped tables. Here, Morita has created more illuminating Japanese details, including custom-made oil lamps topped by shades printed with landscape photography and calligraphy. This technique is also integrated into the dining counter in the ground-floor space, where the counter surface of Japanese cypress is gently illuminated by a backlit panel of graphic paper printed with the ephemeral image of a sea of clouds in Japan.

At first glance Megu Midtown, with its colossal lampshades, appears to be all about making a big, bold design statement, but look a little further into the light and Japanese beauty appears in the most subliminal of places.

TOP LEFT
The ground-floor dining counter with its illuminated panel displaying a sea of clouds.

BOTTOM LEFT
Oil lamps light the predominantly black bar interior.

RIGHT
A mirrored wall in the private dining room is decorated with obi sashes that have been woven through clear acrylic sheets.

LEFT
An antique wedding
pagoda punctures the
double-height central
courtyard.

RIGHT
Antique and hand-
carved timber is enriched
by vibrant colours.

The New York-based, Alsatian-born chef Jean-Georges Vongerichten has come a long way since he arrived in America in 1985. So far, in fact, that author Jay McInerney wrote in *New York Magazine* (27 June, 2005): 'It's probably safe to say that in the past two decades, no single chef has had more influence on the way New Yorkers dine out – or on the way other chefs cook and other restaurants look.' Vongerichten certainly has had plenty of opportunity to influence the culinary scene. Since opening Jo Jo in 1991 he has nurtured a culinary empire with no fewer than 16 restaurants around the world and eight concentrated in Manhattan. Spice Market, his homage to South-east Asian street food, opened just below Soho House in the Meatpacking district in 2004.

Vongerichten has employed a roster of successful designers to create his restaurant interiors; David Rockwell was responsible for Vong, Mercer Kitchen was by Christian Liaigre and both 66 and his latest venture, Perry Street, were Richard Meier productions. For Spice Market, Vongerichten chose Jacques Garcia, the prolific Parisian interior designer responsible for numerous hotels and restaurants worldwide, including Hôtel Costes and the Ladurée tearooms in Paris. Blessed with a soaring 1,115 square metre (12,000 square foot) warehouse, Garcia has created an exotic two-tiered Far Eastern temple replete with teak floors sourced from an ancient 200-year-old Mumbai palace, ornate, carved teak screens and decorative artefacts imported from Rajasthan, South India, Burma and Malaysia.

The palatial feel is enhanced by the internal layout in which the airy ground-floor dining area is punctured by a large central double-height courtyard seating 200 diners. This houses the stairway connecting the two floors and affords diners a view of the basement lounge bar below. Garcia's dramatic centrepiece is a towering antique wedding pagoda integrated into the staircase to form a theatrical threshold for guests to pass through. This is flanked by four lace, silk and Swarovski-crystal cylindrical lanterns. Suspended from the ceiling, these pierce through the two levels, emphasizing the grandeur of the space.

White leather club chairs and sofas, custom-made in a colonial style, add a touch of elegance, while additional seating in the form of Thai wood and Chinese porcelain garden stools adds to the mix. But it's Garcia's vibrant colour palette that really brings the interior to life – antique timber stained shades of turquoise, deep red walls, and Lelièvre fabric drapes of warm orange, ochre and jade green convey a nostalgic sense of the East.

LEFT
The rocky mist marble
sushi bar with its LED-
lit video backdrop.

ABOVE
Rose-coloured glass
frontage etched with
barcode stripes
separates Shibuya
from the casino
circulation routes.

RIGHT
The fiery Tepanyaki
Grill room.

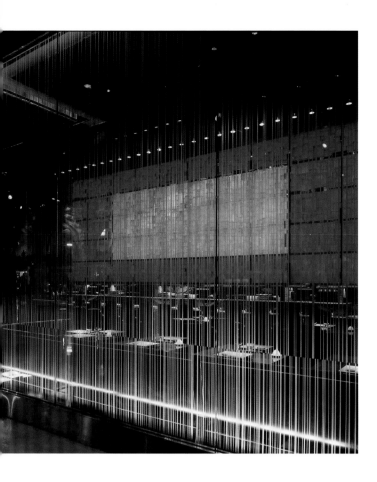

'We wanted to move away from the traditional notions of Japanese design: washed river stones, natural materials and shoji screens,' say Toronto- and New York-based design firm Yabu Pushelberg of Shibuya restaurant. 'We wanted to show the Japan of today – the dichotomies of modern life, the intensity of big cities. They have a different sense of colour in Japan, but Japanese restaurants in North America always seem to have neutral colour schemes.' By contrast, Shibuya is full of colour and texture. From the rose-coloured glass frontage, etched with barcode stripes, and the warm rosewood flooring and tabletops, to colour-changing LED walls and kaleidoscopic video screens, the interior evokes twenty-first century Tokyo with just a touch of the organic, ancient Japan.

Specialists in hospitality design, Glenn Pushelberg and George Yabu have designed the interiors of many hotels and notable restaurants, including Blue Fin in New York and Simon Restaurant in Los Angeles. For Shibuya, they were asked to integrate a sushi bar, dining room, semi-private dining salon and tepanyaki grills into a 650 square metre (7,000 square foot) space in the MGM Grand Hotel and Casino. The 15.2 metre (50 foot) long Sushi Bar, made of rocky mist marble with

a LED-lit video wall backdrop, is the glowing heart of the interior, positioned so that it is clearly visible through the etched glazing that separates Shibuya from the general circulation routes of the hotel and casino.

Yabu Pushelberg have used sculptural partitions by artist Hirotoshi Sawada to divide up the space while at the same time allowing views throughout the restaurant. These organic screens, composed of undulating strips, take on circular shapes, suspended around tables, and also floor-to-ceiling vertical forms, both functioning to create a sense of intimacy between tables. Combined with Dennis Lin's roughly carved timber floor lights, which emit randomly dispersed light, they make for a texturally rich interior. An illuminated opaque acrylic wall, featuring irregularly placed strips of pine that glow a warm orange, separates the dining area from the Tepanyaki Grill. With hot pink lights and stainless steel canopies suspended above glossy rosewood tables, the Tepanyaki Grill is encased in light. In contrast to the moodier main space, this smaller room radiates fiery light and warmth.

Manhattan's historic Meatpacking district is rapidly becoming the neighbourhood of the mega-restaurant. Following in the footsteps of Jean-Georges Vongerichten, who opened Spice Market in 2004, Philadelphia restaurateur Stephen Starr recently opened the 1,486 square metre (16,000 square foot) Buddakan (see pages 94–9) and the 1,115 square metre (12,000 square foot) Morimoto. Just a few blocks away Jean-Yves Haouzi opened the 1,200 square metre (13,000 square foot) Buddha-Bar in April 2006. For the New York outpost of the ten-year-old Paris original, Haouzi gave the Manhattan-based Dupoux Design a $10 million budget to create the Asian-themed restaurant and lounge in a vast warehouse space.

Dupoux Design founder Stephane Dupoux has ten years' experience in creating hip hospitality venues, which include the original Nikki Beach in Miami and the boutique club Cielo in New York. Buddha-Bar is their largest nocturnal venue to date, and Dupoux granted the space an even more impressive scale by inserting a 10.6 metre (35 foot) high

skylight designed by Didi Pei, son of I.M. Pei and head of Pei Partnership Architects in New York. This lofty addition crowns the central dining area, allowing plenty of headroom for an iconic 5 metre (17 foot) high black Buddha, clearly defined against a shimmering wall of gold leaf. 'There are lots of gold Buddhas, but for New York City I wanted the Buddha to be a little bit different, so I went for a black Buddha, especially because New York City is such a cultural melting pot,' explains Dupoux.

The Buddha, basking in a golden glow, is the first view to confront diners after they pass through a dramatic bamboo-lined tunnel guarded by antique Buddha statuettes imported from Thailand. 'The idea is to drive patrons with an increasing energy as they walk in. The arched entranceway is like entering a cave and each Buddha greeting you represents a different wish,' says Dupoux.

The 554-capacity space is divided into three interconnecting sections: the lounge bar, a central dining room and a dining room and sushi bar.

These areas are separated by partitions constructed from rolls of dark brown bamboo scrolls. The scrolls are stacked to form open arches, allowing views and access through the space. The Buddha is book-ended by two raised platforms housing four dining 'pagodas', each of which accommodates eight. Diners are seated on low chairs, with a sunken central well providing leg room. 'It is such a huge space but I didn't want to create rooms within that,' says Dupoux. 'The places that I create are all about seeing and being seen, so you don't want to isolate anyone, but allow everyone to be able to see everyone else. So anywhere in the restaurant you can see across the room, but even if you only have 100 people in there you still don't feel by yourself.'

The two bars at opposite sides of the room – one serving drinks, the other sushi – are both defined by three semi-circular arches that mirror each other and reinforce the Asian theme, lending a sense of symmetry and balance. Buddha-Bar is predominantly full of rich, opulent colours and fabrics, with a dominating palette of dark brown, gold and

ABOVE
Authentic masks imported from Taiwan, Japan and China watch over the sushi bar.

RIGHT
Arches allow for premium people-watching.

LEFT
Circles and arches reinforce the Far-Eastern aesthetic in the lounge bar.

RIGHT
The dining pagodas.

FAR RIGHT
Curved walls were built to keep the energy flowing back into the room.

BELOW
Plan: 1. entrance, 2. lounge deck, 3. buddha gallery, 4. toilets, 5. kitchen, 6. main dining area, 7. sushi bar, 8. lounge bar, 9. Buddha.

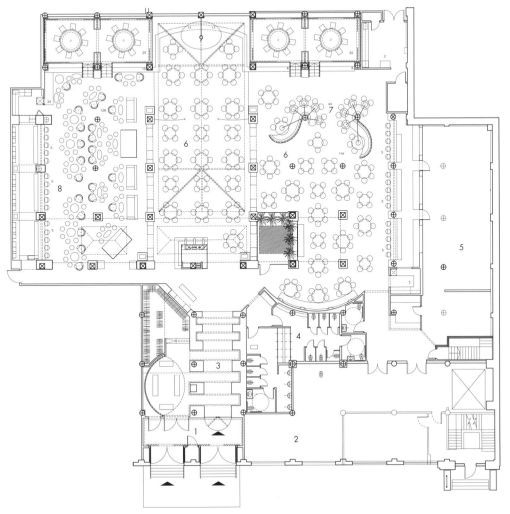

burgundy. The sushi bar, by contrast, features a façade of stacked tempered glass lit with a blue LED in keeping with the marine theme. This is augmented by the back bar display of three aquaria containing jellyfish and lit by LEDs that change colour.

A clever solution to America's smoking ban is the internal courtyard, open to the sky but encased in glass and decorated by an ornamental border of slender trunks and twisted vines. Dupoux says, 'one of the concerns of the local community was the prospect of so many people going outside the restaurant to smoke and then causing an obstruction and disturbing the residents.' By creating this courtyard no one is forced to go outside, keeping the party firmly under one Buddha.

North America's fastest growing metropolis, Las Vegas is reinventing itself once more. Forget the outlandish theming of past decades – such confections are being usurped by high design, and within each existing hotel, casual and themed food outlets are being replaced by stylish restaurants boasting superstar chefs that could rival anything New York or London has to offer. The Mirage, originally opened by Vegas entrepreneur Steven Wynn in 1989, underwent a significant renovation between 2005 and 2006 to make the hotel 'chic and contemporary'. Fin was part of this makeover. The 92-seat Chinese restaurant is located next door to Stack (designed by Graft), and opened in November 2005.

Keen to avoid using 'typical Chinese-inspired references or general Asian themes', prolific restaurant, hotel and retail designers Yabu Pushelberg aimed for an interior that 'walks the fine line between edgy and elegant, with a sophisticated medley of past and present'. As with many of their schemes, the designers collaborated with independent artists to create a texturally rich and animated space. In contrast to the bright vibrancy of their design for the multiple-roomed Shibuya (see pages 28–9), for Fin Yabu Pushelberg opted for a subtle, sophisticated colour palette of gold and jade with rich dark accents, as befits a more intimate, formal dining room.

Roughly octagonal, with a symmetrical layout and high ceilings, the restaurant allows entering guests a clear view through the room to Hirotoshi Sawada's geometric sculpture, suspended above a silver statue of a rearing horse and water feature. Framing this view are strings of translucent resin spheres by artist Helen Poon, cascading down from the ceiling like amber beads (and reminiscent of the glass bubbles at Patrick Jouin's Mix; see pages 150–53). These are aligned alongside tables, lending a hint of privacy between diners.

The main dining area is flanked by two octagonal, private dining salons, concealed behind artworks. The left salon is housed within translucent silk panels painted with traditional Chinese images of blossom branches. The salon on the right is screened off by a mural painted on copper wire mesh, which is layered with laser-cut acrylic, forming an atmospheric backdrop that resembles misty, golden mountains.

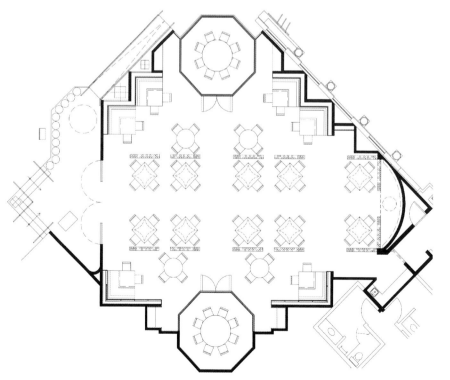

FAR LEFT
Evocations of China are subtly integrated in the form of blossom designs on silk panels and a mountain mural.

ABOVE
Sawada's geometric wall and the rearing silver horse provide a central focus.

LEFT
Plan showing the two octagonal private dining salons at opposite sides of the room.

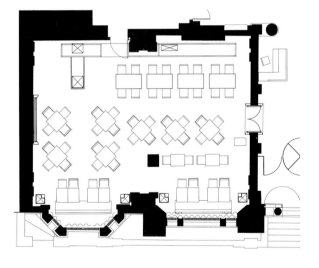

ABOVE
Plan of the compact,
64-seat dining room.

LEFT
The bronze-framed
display cabinet is backlit
to illuminate the amber,
deep red and moss green
glass panelling.

TOP LEFT
Simple Asian ceramics
decorate the shelves like
organic sculptures.

TOP RIGHT
Burnt-orange silkscreened
butterflies adorn two
walls.

New York-based architect and designer Jeffrey Beers leapt at the opportunity to design his first London project – the interiors for entrepreneur Robert Earl's Fifty, a private members club and casino complex in the genteel surroundings of St James's. Originally built in the 1820s and designed by architect Benjamin Watt, the property has a long history as a gentleman's club and casino, and was apparently once known as 'the Ascot of gambling.' Earl's twenty-first-century revamp, which opened in April 2005, includes two fine-dining restaurants: V, serving gourmet French food, and Rama, specializing in pan-Asian fare. Both are overseen by renowned chef and restaurateur Jean-Georges Vongerichten. In terms of design, Rama, the 64-seat ground-floor restaurant, is the more interesting of the two.

Restricted from altering the listed nineteenth-century interiors, Beers has taken advantage of the palatial proportions and, inspired by exotic fruits, spices and flowers of Asia, imbued the 110 square metre (1,200 square foot) room with warmth through his use of decorative pattern. Two walls are covered in a bespoke, silk-screened fabric bearing a bold burnt-orange butterfly motif (the restaurant takes its name from the Malay word for butterfly, 'ramarama'). Meanwhile, the rear wall is 'painted' by a geometric collage of amber, deep red and moss green coloured

transparent glass panels, which are framed within a bronze structure and backlit to create a glowing cabinet that showcases simple, white Asian chinaware.

'I was really trying to get a deep and rich saturation of colour,' says Beers, who likes to explore the magical properties of glass and is particularly influenced by the work of Dale Chihuly. 'He probably has the most exuberant colour sense of any artist I've ever known in my life – this bold, emotional kind of creative stamina, phenomenal colour.' In keeping with this rich, burnished palette, floors are dark ipe wood, table tops are ebonized lacewood and seating is upholstered in reds and taupes, while banquettes are covered in a colourful floral pattern by Kenzo.

Describing his design approach, Beers, who has been creating hospitality venues for more than 20 years, says: 'The ultimate goal for me is to deliver magic, something the guest has never seen before. I strive for my projects be stimulating and memorable, not just my particular stamp of design. I use my own tricks and signature elements to achieve this; my projects are never stark or minimalistic, they are quite rich from a materiality and a colour standpoint; they've always got quite a lot going on in them.'

SEOUL SOUL
YAMAGATA JAPAN ZOKEI-SYUDAN

LEFT
Colourful illuminated
cubes, which act as a
design motif
throughout, can be
seen here supporting
the grand central table
for six.

RIGHT
Seoul Soul's brightly
lit façade.

Okinawa-born architect and designer Yusaku Kaneshiro founded his Tokyo-based agency Zokei-Syudan in 2000. The output of his tiny four-strong team has been prolific, with the company responsible for more than 500 restaurants and bars in Japan. Generally employing an organic aesthetic, Kaneshiro's aim is to create 'something that doesn't exist, that no-one has seen before'. As a result, his interiors often resemble something a little other worldly, sci-fi or even futuristically post-apocalyptic.

Seoul Soul differs somewhat from the agency's more rustic interiors, but nevertheless exhibits a strong Zokei-Syudan approach. The long, narrow space is divided into intriguing dining pockets and cocoons on varying levels, with traditional antique elements and an eclectic selection of lighting. The small Korean restaurant and bar is situated in a historic district of Yamagata, a city located just under three hours by express train from Toyko. The 268 square metre (2,885 square foot)

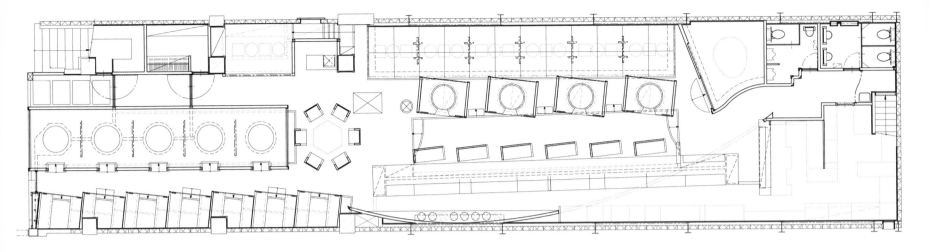

site was previously a games arcade. 'The budget was limited,' say Zokei-Syudan, 'so we made it as gorgeous as possible while using cheap materials'. The new restaurant opened in December 2004.

There are a series of dining compartments, arranged in rows throughout the interior. The main body of the room comprises a bar counter-positioned along a sweeping wall decorated with Korean characters in relief. Running parallel to the bar is a raised catwalk supporting large illuminated cube structures that display multi-coloured stripes, lending a touch of fairground kitsch. Accessible from this raised platform are four dining compartments, backed with wire mesh to maintain views through to the other side. Small steps between the dining booths provide access back down to the ground-level area, which houses a row of six low circular tables for two. These are separated by matching upright circular antique cabinets and lit from above by a glowing canopy of lanterns, all duplicated by a mirrored wall that maximizes the sense of space.

Towards the front of the restaurant Kaneshiro has created a raised room within the room, in the form of a long, timber-lined salon privé accommodating five large tables. Red velvet drapes between tables provide privacy. Parallel to this are a series of seven darker and more intimate raised dining compartments. Those who fancy being the centre of attention might, however, prefer dining below the large crystal chandelier at the hexagonal glass-topped table in the centre of the restaurant. This table for six – with its base of internally illuminated multi-coloured Mondrianesque cubes – resembles an art installation.

ABOVE
The plan shows how, in typical Zokei-Syudan style, the restaurant is divided up into various dining compartments and cocoons.

LEFT
Tables for two are separated by circular antique cabinets, which are reflected in the mirrored wall.

RIGHT
The featured lighting has a touch of the retro 1960s-meets-gaudy fairground about it.

YAUATCHA

LONDON UK CHRISTIAN LIAIGRE

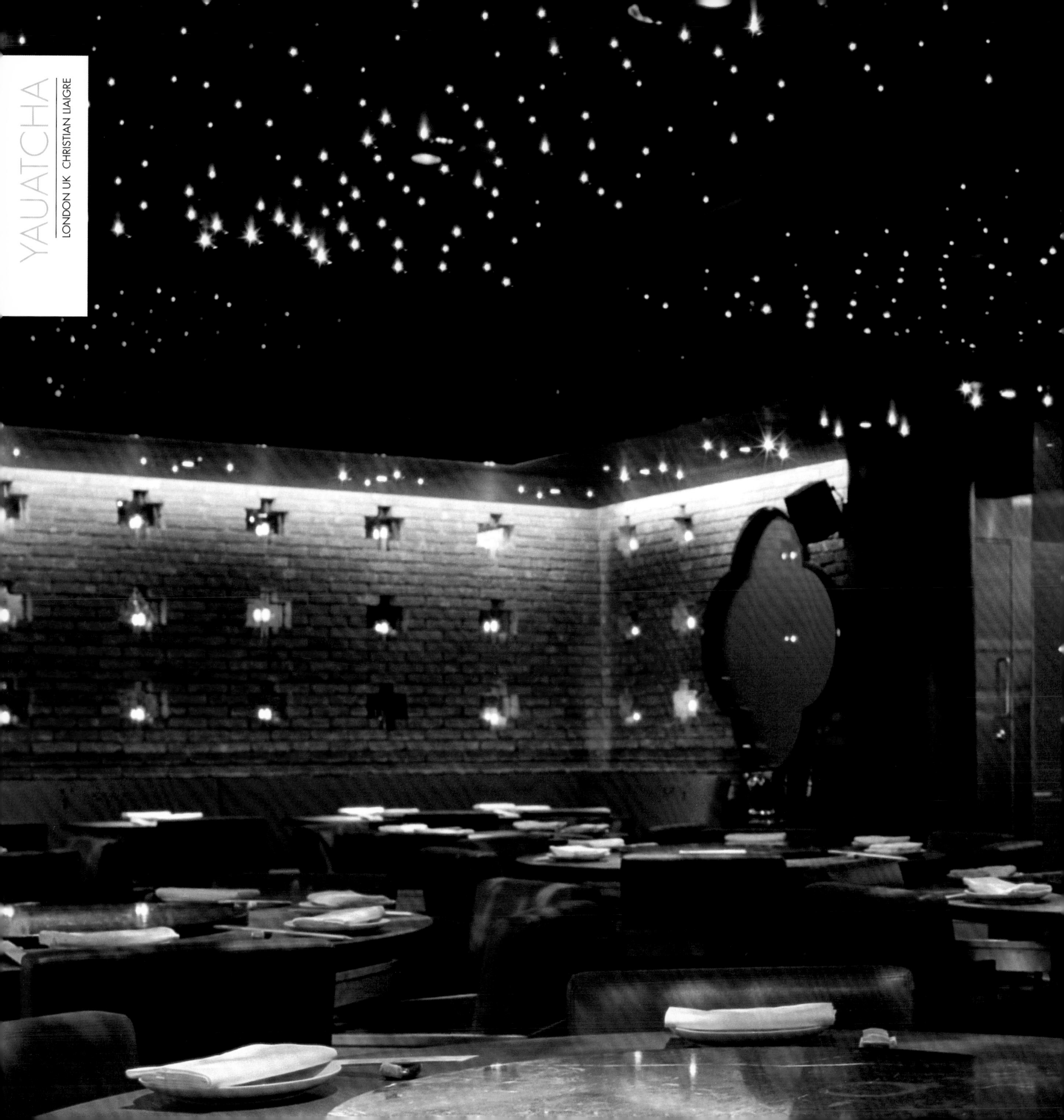

London restaurateur Alan Yau needs little introduction. The Hong Kong-born maverick has come a long way since creating the minimalist communal dining Wagamama concept during the 1990s. Having sold the now international chain in 1997, Yau didn't rest on his laurels. Instead, he swiftly teamed up with French designer Christian Liaigre, whom he commissioned to design the communal, informal, no-bookings policy Thai restaurant Busaba Eathai, of which there are now several in London. A far more ambitious project followed in 2001 – the rather spectacular Hakkasan. This moody subterranean temple to Far Eastern chic in London's West End has an imposing Liaigre interior replete with antique timber screens imported from Taipei. It scooped a Michelin star for its modern Cantonese food and dim sum within just two years of opening.

Three years later, in March 2004, Yau unveiled his next creation, a contemporary Chinese teahouse combined with a dim sum restaurant. Rumoured to have cost £4.2 million, it occupies the ground floor and basement of Richard Rogers Partnership's brand new Igeni building in Soho. Yauatcha's glass corner façade is an arresting sight, with displays of distinctive pink and green packaging and a deep blue tropical aquarium lining one side. The ground-floor tea house and patisserie clearly differs from Hakkasan in its café style setting, light surfaces of white carrara marble and terrazzo and abundance of natural light. However, it does share core design components with the earlier restaurant, such as accent colours, blue glass and embroidered details (for example pink cherry blossom) on the leatherwork of the grey stained American-elm.

At Yauatcha the ground-floor tea parlour and basement dim sum restaurant were – after three design drafts – conceived as opposites, like day and night. Yau broke the mould by creating an all day dim sum restaurant, since it is traditionally considered a lunchtime meal. Descending into the restaurant is like entering a twilight zone – the antithesis of the tea house – with black terrazzo floors and stronger accent colours, such as the exotic turquoise leather of the perimeter banquettes. Lacking the ceiling height of Hakkasan, Liaigre created atmosphere and drama through clever use of lighting. The interior walls are clad in handmade French brick with cross-shaped apertures that twinkle with faux candles and generate a slightly catacomb-cum-ecclesiastical feel. A starry canopy overhead, sprinkled with sparkly fibre-optics, adds an element of disco glam.

The signature blue glass makes an appearance in the tropical aquarium housed within the bar counter, which has windows shaped like stylized four-leaf clovers (a popular motif often found in Asian gardens), and in the translucent window along one side of the room which allows misty views of the dim sum chefs at work. Despite Yauatcha attracting numerous celebrity diners – from Uma Thurman to Gordon Ramsay – Yau remains characteristically modest: 'We don't chase an in-crowd. The customers have to come to you. All you can do it set out your stall and hope that enough people find your proposition sufficiently intriguing and enjoyable to come back and bring their friends.' Proof of its success was swift; Yauatcha was awarded a Michelin star within six months of opening.

THIS PAGE

LEFT
Authenticity is in the
details, from lanterns
to elaborate
carvings and Zelij
tilework.

RIGHT
An illuminated pool
is the central focus.

OVERLEAF

TOP LEFT
Detailed
architectural
drawings show the
Islamic arches and
tilework.

BOTTOM LEFT
The plan reveals the
pattern of the
marble floor and
pool tiles.

RIGHT
Laser-cut lanterns
cast a starry
light around this
dining salon.

Moroccan-themed restaurants and bars have been popular in cities such as London, New York and Paris for quite a while, but few have been executed with as much intricate care and attention as Dar El Yacout in central Milan. This three-storey restaurant, tea-room and lounge bar is modelled on a Moroccan riad, and just months after opening in November 2004 was already hosting prestigious fashion week parties for the likes of Donatella Versace. Restaurateur Antonio Moscara purchased an abandoned building in 2001 and commissioned Studio Carratta to undertake what was a substantial restoration of the property. 'After many journeys to Morocco we decided that everything had to be absolutely original and as luxurious as possible to satisfy the growing enthusiasm in Milan about this particular venture,' explains project architect Pasquale Saturno Carratta.

The name Dar El Yacout translates as 'there where the most precious diamonds are' and no expense was spared – the project cost 7 million Euros – to create a lavish interior rich with Moroccan colours, mosaics, crafts and carved details. The 900 square metre (9,688 square foot) interior comprises the ground-floor lounge, Salon Bacha, which is furnished with sofas for drinking aperitifs and relaxing with narghilés (hookah pipes), and

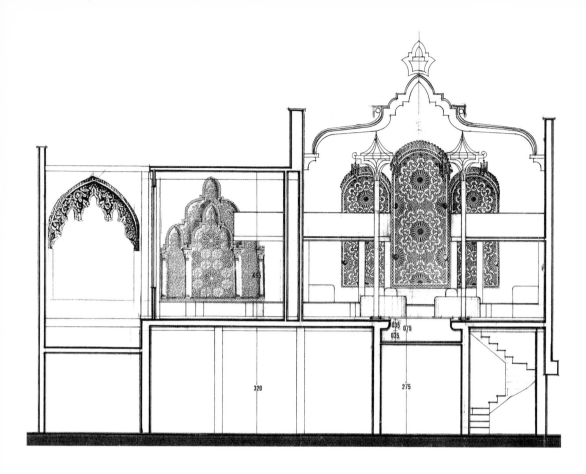

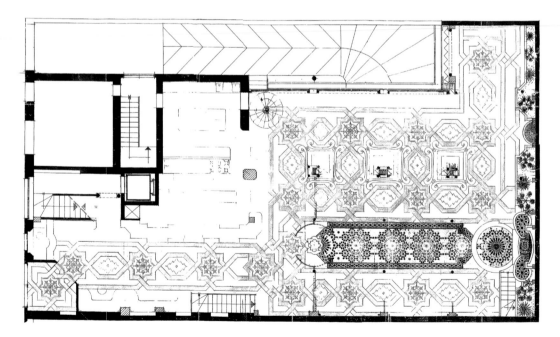

a dining area called Salon Marocaine. The glowing focal point is an internally illuminated pool arranged below an open, double-height courtyard, which is overlooked by the second floor and boasts a stunning display of exquisite Zelij tilework. On the mezzanine floor, between the two balconies, is a lounge bar and on the third floor the Salon Privé.

So keen were the architects to achieve utter authenticity in their interior that they studied Moroccan design in depth; the geometry of the inlaid marble flooring, archwork and Zelij patterns is faithful to Islamic tradition. As they say of the vibrant tilework, everything is symbolic and imbued with meaning: 'We understand that every single little tile is the protagonist of a virtual army which starts from the centre (the King), and which extends around in a radial way ready to defend him (knights, bishops, knaves and so on), all following the shape of a star.'

Even the typical yellow stone (carparo) and oxide pigments were imported directly from Morocco to attain the perfect colour scheme. 'We used colours from the Moroccan flag,' says Pasquale Saturno. '"Earth red" is the same colour used for façades in Marrakech. This is mixed with "palmerie green", symbolizing oasis and rest, and "egg yellow" representing the colour of the sun. The blue represents the blue that is everywhere in the Middle East, representing water, wellness, rest, life – or alternatively, sky, destiny, the divine. For this reason we used blue in the Salon Privé and for the more exclusive areas.'

A variety of lighting enhances the atmosphere, including colourful glass lamps, impressive ceiling lanterns of laser-cut steel shipped from Casablanca, and wall lanterns that radiate glittering, textured light. Most spectacular is the starry 'Arabian sky' of fibre-optics decorating the blue and gold dome that crowns the space.

NEW BAROQUE

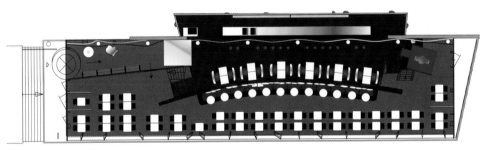

Dining out is often likened to a theatrical experience, with 'show kitchens' providing drama and restaurant interiors resembling sets where diners make an entrance and indulge in good old-fashioned voyeurism while chowing down. Blits restaurant on the river Maas in Rotterdam opened in September 2005 and is the whimsical Dutch designer Marcel Wanders's tribute to this concept. 'As evening falls it's time for the audience to take to the stage,' he writes. 'Spectators and theatre merge and it becomes impossible to tell the actors from the onlookers. The stage is scattered with props, and the formalities of the performance make way for chance encounters and unwritten romances. Laughter fills the room, and the pressures of the day make way for the sensuality of the night.'

The theatrical theme evolved in response to the host structure, built in 1989 and designed by architect Francine Houben. At that time it was an important new build, radically altering the character of Rotterdam's landscape. Wanders explains, 'Rotterdam was rebuilt very quickly following World War II and had been positioned so that the city had its back to the water.' During the early nineties the city planners launched a new master plan that involved redressing this with waterside developments. According to Wanders, this was one of the first examples, built on the river shore to face the water: 'at the time I lived in the city and remember it as a remarkable development.'

Although thrilled to be asked to create a restaurant in the then redundant space – which had previously housed a restaurant – Wanders found the property's assets were also its flaws. "It's mainly glass so there's a spectacular view and it's fantastic to see the boats on the water and enjoy the sunshine but this is a reason to go once, not to return. For a restaurant to be successful you need an interesting interior too and this is where all the glass work becomes a problem, on a rainy or grey, misty day – which, to be honest, we have a few of in Holland – it's not so nice.'

Presented with this dilemma, Wanders began to consider the restaurant's relationship with the water as that between the audience and stage, 'but I liked the idea of reversing that, as if the audience were on the water and the diners are the performers with the restaurant the stage.' Wanders created two curved tiers of seating and maintained the glass façade bordering the water, but closed off sections of the rear façade with bold symbolic gestures: large curtains, a gaudy floral backdrop and transparent yellow film affixed to the glazing behind the bar. 'We wanted to create the atmosphere of being on stage, so the big bouquet is like one that has been thrown onto the stage after the premiere,' says Wanders. 'Also the yellow film creates a warm glow, so even on a cold, misty day you feel like the sun is shining outside – this is important.'

Typically Wanders is the glossy red Love Suite with its heart-shaped window. Never one to miss the opportunity for romance, or to explore the evocative emotional possibilities of design, Wanders describes this salon for two as a castle, or love nest. 'It's the place where the lovers would sing their big aria,' he says. Although initially the plan was to create a room for blind dates, Wanders realized couples on a blind date are far too nervous to be perched on high in a private room, and so it is instead aimed at couples celebrating anniversaries. 'We all have moments when we want to do something special, and this is the place. You can close the curtains if you want to be intimate, but we don't want things to get too crazy of course – it's just a little fun game.'

As for the name, it was chosen by the owners. 'In Holland, about 30 years ago "blits" meant what we now call "cool", it was like "Wow, that's so cool". They loved the word and wanted the name to appeal to young people with a reasonable amount of money to spend, and to reflect a restaurant that wasn't too high end or uptight, but a place where for a good price you can have a great time.'

PREVIOUS PAGE

LEFT
Two tiers of dining tables curve around the space, giving prime views of the water.

TOP RIGHT
The audience's view of Wanders's dining 'stage'.

BOTTOM RIGHT
The restaurant seats about 138, including room for two in the Love Suite (the red box to the right of the plan).

THIS PAGE

TOP LEFT
A heart-shaped window into the glossy Love Suite.

ABOVE
Curtains can be drawn to make dining à deux a private affair.

RIGHT
Blits is positively blooming with this giant bouquet photomural.

CHÂTEAU RESTAURANT

TOKYO JAPAN GLAMOROUS

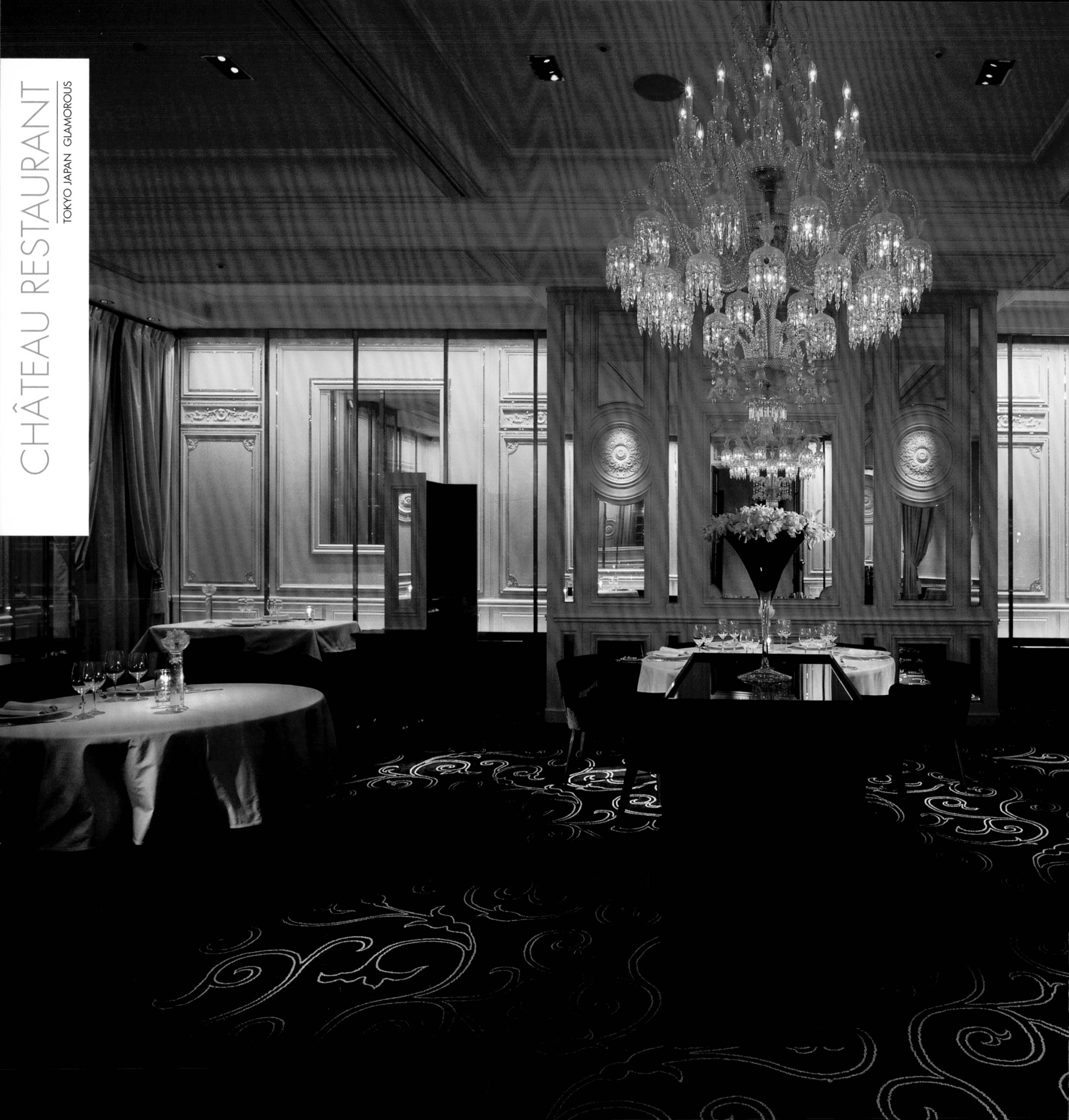

Designing a restaurant for legendary French chef Joël Robuchon sounds like a daunting prospect, after all this is the man named Cuisinier du Siècle (Chef of the Century) in 1990 by the influential Gault-Millau guide. Despite receiving this honour he famously retired from his Michelin three-star eponymous Parisian restaurant in 1996, only to return to the stoves in 2003 with his new, more casual, no-booking dining concept L'Atelier de Robuchon, also located in Paris but inspired by both Spanish and Japanese cuisines.

Since then Robuchon has swiftly nurtured an international empire, opening a L'Atelier and the fine-dining restaurant The Mansion in what is fast becoming one of the world's new capitals of gourmet, Las Vegas, as well as outposts in London, New York, Monte Carlo and Tokyo. Who better to design the Tokyo branch – Château Restaurant Joël Robuchon – than Yasumichi Morita and his Glamorous team, who have created numerous projects in Japan as well as the stunning New York restaurant Megu.

Château is located in one of Tokyo's most popular shopping and eating destinations, the Yebisu Garden Place, a multi-purpose district described as a city within a city, in the Ebisu neighbourhood next to Roppongi and Shibuya.

LEFT
The smarter, more formal dining room of Joël Robuchon.

ABOVE RIGHT
Decorative mouldings, encased behind glass, twinkle with crystal chips.

RIGHT
Ground-floor plan. 1. entrance, 2. toilets, 3. La Table.

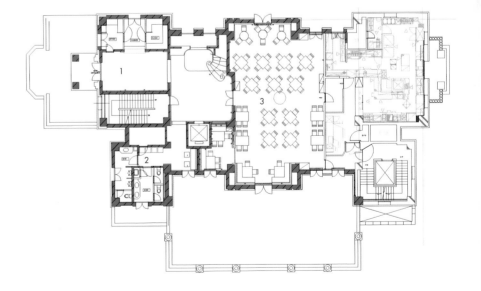

The establishment features walls transported from a French château – hence the name – and comprises four distinct areas; a boulangerie and patisserie called La Boutique, La Table, Joël Robuchon and the Rouge Bar. Glamorous refurbished La Table, an 87-cover dining room on the ground floor and two spaces on the first floor, the 58-cover Joël Robuchon and the Rouge Bar.

Morita drew his inspiration from Robuchon's 'elegant and modern' cuisine and the result is more classical than many of Glamorous's previous works. Visual continuity is ensured by the distinctive swirling design of the bespoke carpet, which remains the same throughout but appears in different two-tone colour combinations for each of the spaces. Baccarat crystal chandeliers add a touch of decadence to both dining rooms, however Morita has created slightly different atmospheres in each of the spaces by employing subtle variations in the design.

Joël Robuchon is distinguished as the smarter dining room by virtue of classic champagne-gold walls, white linen and armchairs, whereas the more relaxed dining room, La Table, is furnished with undressed polished rosewood tables and modern leather chairs with violet walls. Decorative details in both rooms include crystal doorknobs affixed to the walls, but beyond that they differ again. La Table is enlivened by two bold abstract artworks, whereas Joël Robuchon is given a sparkle of glamour with glittering crystal chips embedded into the decorative moldings of the walls so they catch the light. These walls are encased behind clear glass.

In the first floor Rouge Bar Morita chose Robuchon's signature colours – red and black – to create a small but theatrical 22-seat space. Red walls and velvet drapes, combined with furniture upholstered in black mohair and a highly polished black granite bar counter, create a richly textured environment. It is the lighting, one of Morita's specialities, that steals the show – two bespoke black crystal chandeliers cascade down over the bar injecting that signature Glamorous touch.

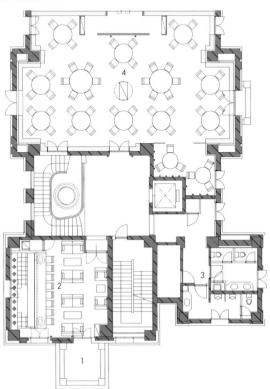

TOP LEFT
Contemporary abstract art decorates La Table.

LEFT
First-floor plan.
1. terrace, 2. Rouge Bar, 3. toilets, 4. Joël Robuchon.

RIGHT
Decadent and plush, the Rouge Bar features typically Glamorous lighting.

NEW YORK USA   PATRICK JOUIN

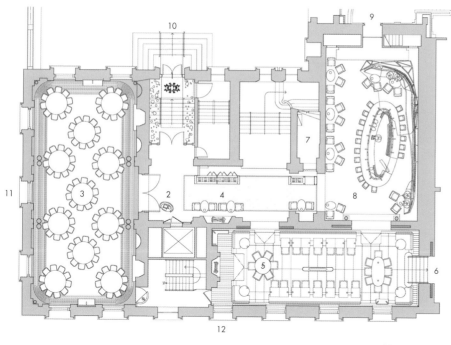

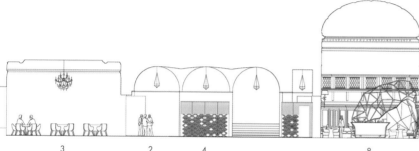

3   2   4   8

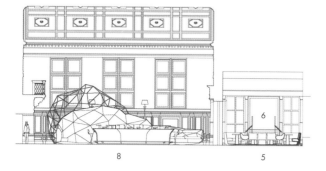

8   5

KEY

1   Restaurant entrance
2   Greeter's desk
3   Madison banquet room
4   Wine display
5   Dining room
6   Kitchens
7   Cloakroom
8   Gold Room bar
9   Hotel lobby
10   Villard Mansion courtyard
11   Madison Avenue
12   50th street

THIS PAGE

FAR LEFT
Intricate mosaics decorate the original groin-vaulted ceiling.

LEFT
From top: plan and sections. The 370 square metre (4,000 square foot) space comprises three areas; the bar, a fine-dining room and an events space.

RIGHT
Mirrored pebbles sprinkle the entrance steps.

NEXT PAGE

LEFT
Lighting recessed into the foot-rail sets the Corian bar aglow.

RIGHT
The caramel-hued chairs in the panelled fine-dining room were custom-designed by Jouin for Gilt and manufactured by Laval.

Young Parisian designer Patrick Jouin has blazed an exciting trail across the globe by creating spectacular restaurants for the burgeoning empire of Michelin-starred French chef Alain Ducasse. Spoon Byblos in St Tropez and Plaza Athénée in Paris were both showcased in the forerunner to this book, *Restaurant Design* and Mix in Las Vegas appears in this volume (see pages 150–53). Although his most visually stunning project is probably Mix, with a brand new interior, Jouin is well-practised in the art of creating contemporary restaurants within listed, historic interiors – Gilt is one such project.

Located in the nineteenth-century Villard Mansion wing of the New York Palace Hotel in Manhattan, Gilt occupies the space that previously housed the legendary, Adam D. Tihany-designed Le Cirque. No traces of this colourful antecedent remain – instead the original nineteenth-century decorative intricacies of stained-glass windows, ornate mosaic ceilings, decorative plasterwork and refined wood panelling

provide the magnificent historic setting for Jouin's designs. Armed with a budget of $4.5 million, Jouin has created a 52-cover boutique dining room and an adjoining bar that seats 44 people in two interconnecting rooms. The restaurant, which opened in December 2005, initially served the avant-garde gourmet French food of English-born chef Paul Liebrandt, but he was replaced in September 2006 by a new chef – Christopher Lee – and menu serving modern American food.

The restaurant entrance is independent of the hotel and situated on the side of the courtyard, accessible from Madison Avenue. Original, white mosaic-tiled stairs are sprinkled either side with mirrored glass pebbles, which, when seen up close, reveal distorted reflections of their surroundings. Such delicate embellishment is all that's required as the stairs lead into an impressive original hallway with a groin-vaulted mosaic ceiling. The only sign of modernity here is Jouin's sleek, grey-tinted glass wine display

and glimpses through a doorway ahead of the colourful, LED-lit 'oyster shell' of the bar.

Jouin's fondness for grand visual gestures is clearly present in Gilt's double-height, barrel-vaulted Gold Room Bar. Taking centre stage is an elegantly curved white oval bar constructed from powder-coated fibreglass supporting a polished Cameo White Corian countertop. At its base, a custom-designed, polished stainless-steel footrail with integrated spotlights sets this focal point aglow. Rising behind it, like some kind of futuristic glacier, or multi-faceted illuminous crystal rock, is Jouin's abstract 'oyster shell'.

The upper section of this freestanding, hand-carved structure is left exposed, revealing a geometric skeleton of fibreglass-coated American black walnut, reminiscent of the silvery strands of an imperfect spider's web. The lower section is concealed by a rock-like covering. The exterior of these fibreglass-coated timber panels is finished with glossy chrome paint and the concave interior surrounding the bar is upholstered with a bronze Sharkskin fabric by Kvadrat, lit from below by an LED lightbox to radiate different colours. A pair of tables is integrated within the deepest curve of the shell. Banquette seating is upholstered with bronze leather, in keeping with the

shell's interior surface and glass-topped tables, incorporating tea-light lamps, reflecting the changing hues of the LED lighting.

Access to the dining room is via the main hallway or an interconnecting doorway from the bar. A lower ceiling height, combined with carved and gilded, rich dark wood panelling and heavy red drapes at the windows, serves to create an intimate, rarefied atmosphere well suited to haute cuisine dining. In this imposing space Jouin wisely did little, simply creating an acoustically sophisticated continuous perimeter banquette and a floor system of caramel-coloured Dalsouple rubber. Thus the bench seating, covered in matching caramel brown leather, lines the edges of the room and slopes down to seamlessly join the floor.

Bespoke tables have solid walnut tops but are usually draped in white linen, as befitting a fine-dining restaurant. Dining chairs, which display those characteristic soft Jouin curves, were custom-designed for Gilt and manufactured by Laval. Covered in caramel-hued faux leather, their glinting silver sides of carved, metallic-covered MDF, add a subtle, twenty-first century touch in this otherwise historic space.

LEFT
Exposed brickwork
and Starck's cameos
add a twenty-first-
century edge to the
original dark wood
panelling and ornate
gilt details.

RIGHT
Intimate private
dining in the Pink
Salon.

Who better to create the decadent interiors of luxury crystal manufacturer Baccarat's sumptuous new Paris headquarters but France's most venerated designer extraordinaire Philippe Starck? In typically grandiose style Starck proclaimed of the project: 'To me the gist of Baccarat is a world of illusion originating from the glitter of light on the facets of cut crystal, and it led me to dream up a crystal palace where everything is possible. The interplay of light and crystal turns into mental and poetic games in which everything is relative and subject to illusion. It perfectly corresponds to the attitude I like in life, this deep understanding that all that is relative becomes a supreme way to love and dream.'

Situated on place des Etats-Unis, in the embassy-laden sixteenth arrondissement, Maison de Baccarat opened in 2003. It occupies the former private residence of society queen and arts patron Marie-Laure de Noailles (1902–71) and comprises a boutique selling Baccarat homewares, jewels and accessories, a museum and an exhibition and events space called the Ball Room. Upstairs, reached by a sparkling red carpet inlaid with tiny LEDs, is the petite jewel in the crown, Le Cristal Room, a small but rather stately 47-cover restaurant overseen by chef Thierry Burlot.

Although Baccarat gave Starck carte blanche in Le Cristal Room, he preserved much of the original ornate and gilded interior and with it a sense of history. Formerly the dining room of de Noailles, it is here that the legendary salon hostess entertained the likes of Jean Cocteau, Luis Buñuel, Salvador Dalí and other leading Surrealists alongside aristocrats, diplomats and actors. Lofty proportions, huge mirrors and opulent gilt cornicing lend an inherent grandeur that appears tailormade for displays of Baccarat's exquisite crystal candelabra and chandeliers.

Areas of exposed brick wall, light timber parquet floors, mirrored table tops and bespoke furnishings in delicate shades of grey and pink serve to elevate the imposing, somewhat heavy effects of the dark wood panelling and gilt details. Gazing upwards, diners are treated to a signature eighteenth-century decorative illusion – a trompe l'oeil sky with a Starck twist in which white fluffy clouds drift across a pink sky. Highly polished, reflective metal table tops mirror this image below.

Like Kong, another of Starck's Parisian restaurants, the seat backs of the pink sofas feature portrait cameos. These portray Louis XV – the king responsible for granting the establishment of the first glass-making facility in Baccarat in 1764 – and a woman, who could represent either Marie-Antoinette or possibly the former lady of the house, Marie-Laure de Noailles.

Semi-private dining is provided by the adjoining Pink Salon, a sugary pink boudoir lined by diaphanous white curtains and a padded-silk ceiling, crowned by a majestic black Baccarat crystal chandelier.

Amsterdam-based agency Tjep. was established by Eindhoven Design Academy alumni Frank Tjepkema and Janneke Hooymans in 2001. They started out as product and furniture designers, creating pieces with a discernibly Dutch conceptual sensibility, such as the pre-cracked, unbreakable rubber vase 'Shock Proof', and 'Tak', a seating system for two modelled on a giant bird's nest. Their restaurant interiors are equally playful. Fabbrica opened in October 2005 in Rotterdam harbour, and is the second restaurant for client Vasso Panagoulopoulos. The first was the child-friendly Praq (see pages 168–71).

Asked to create an Italian restaurant, Frank Tjepkema says, 'We always begin by investigating a theme, so with Fabbrica we explored all the clichés and metaphors we could find that relate to Italian restaurants. Also, we were dealing with an old warehouse in Rotterdam harbour and so we let ourselves be inspired by that, inserting industrial elements that relate to that.' Looking to Italy for inspiration, their elementary ingredients include Bisazza mosaic, wood-fired ovens, pastel ice-cream colours and flamboyant pattern. The result is an informal refectory-style restaurant that no doubt works as well by day as night, with an interior constructed from rustic, industrial materials that are given a glamorous edge by baroque patterns, soft pastel colours and crystal chandeliers.

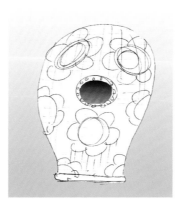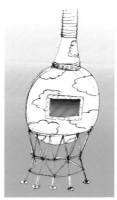

FAR LEFT
Mirrored panels feature oversized baroque patterns taken from Italian wallpaper.

TOP LEFT
Tjep. chose pastel ice-cream colours in keeping with the Italian theme.

TOP RIGHT
Early renderings show chandeliers contrasting with the rustic elements.

ABOVE
A series of sketches for the wood-burning oven.

The existing nineteenth-century warehouse interior was a fundamental influence on the design too: 'We chose not to intervene with the authentic industrial character and so left the original structure intact.' Scrubbed timber floorboards and exposed brick walls provide a warm, almost rural backdrop, brightened and sophisticated by Tjep.'s glossy communal picnic-bench furniture in 1950s 'Italian ice-cream parlour colours' of pink and pistachio green. To the centre of the space a 'floating train structure', incorporating narrow open compartments, features small bench seats and tables suspended from the compartment roof to offer more intimate dining for couples.

Decorative elements are fabulously juxtaposed with simple, industrial materials, such as the robust wood-fired oven. This is particularly resplendent with its outer coating of floral Bisazza mosaic (a pattern also used by Fabio Novembre in the lobby of the Una Hotel Vittoria in Florence) set against a rustic backdrop of timber logs, stored within industrial metal shelving constructed from crane parts. Elsewhere, walls are dressed with large mirror panels etched/layered with oversized florid, fanciful patterns from Italian wallpaper, which create complex reflections and add a superfluous hint of decadence next to the bare brick walls. A series of large crystal chandeliers suspended above the row of communal tables are the final twinkling baroque flourish.

Tjep. conceived the entire project, from the interior to the name itself. 'Fabbrica struck us at the most convenient name,' says Tjepkema. 'Fabbrica means factory in Italian – we envisioned the canteen of a very special factory, a romantic factory where pleasure is produced for guests.'

RIGHT
Shelving units constructed
from crane parts pay
homage to the surrounding
industrial harbour area.

LÁGRIMAS NEGRAS

MADRID SPAIN CHRISTIAN LIAIGRE

LEFT
Oversized timber shutters shield the restaurant interior from the strong Spanish sun.

RIGHT
Pattern is everywhere, most strikingly in the illuminated arabesque design of the bar façade.

FAR RIGHT
Wall coverings of heavy leather are embroidered with the kind of detail found on matador jackets.

BELOW RIGHT
Sketch for the wine cellar display, which houses 4,000 bottles.

BOTTOM RIGHT
Liaigre's sketch for a chair, showing his signature embroidered leatherwork.

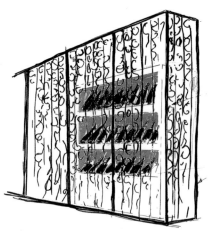

Hotel Puerta América opened to huge fanfare in 2005 and no wonder, as this 76 million Euro hotel was the joint creation of more than 20 international architecture and design superstars; a 'dream team' including such luminaries as Ron Arad, Zaha Hadid and Jean Nouvel. Most were granted an entire floor each to create their own personal vision of what hotel accommodation could dare to be in the twenty-first century. The ground-floor public spaces were divided into a calming minimalist lobby space by John Pawson, a futuristic cocktail bar by Marc Newson and the Lágrimas Negras (Black Tears) restaurant by French designer Christian Liaigre.

Liaigre is internationally known for his distinctive design style, an exotic minimalism characterized by dark timbers and richly dyed leather sofas and chairs often bearing decorative stitching – a look dubbed 'luxe, calme and moderne' by Herbert Ypma, author of *Maison Liaigre* (Thames and Hudson, 2004). Residential schemes are his forte, but he is no stranger to commercial interiors, having created New York's Mercer Hotel and the one-star Michelin restaurant Hakkasan in London (featured in *Restaurant Design*) among others.

Although each of his projects is unmistakeably 'Liaigre' and modern, the designer takes care to pay homage to heritage, of either the location or the food concept. At Lágrimas Negras, a narrow double-height dining room with a bar and café area on the side, the Spanish influences from regions such as Andalusia, Galicia and Catalonia are subtle, integrated and woven into decorative details rather than being overtly thematic. In the absence of colour – the restaurant is predominantly monochromatic and grey – it is these elements that lend Lágrimas Negras its textural richness.

Echoes of ornate wrought ironwork and the intricate embroideries that adorn matador's jackets can be found in the pattern of the heavy grey leather brocade that hangs from ceiling-to-floor to conceal the service areas, and most strikingly in the elaborate arabesque design of the illuminated bar façade, which is constructed from LG Hi-Macs (a durable acrylic solid surface similar to Corian and becoming increasingly popular in commercial environments). The glass and aluminium wine storage display that screens the restaurant from the kitchen also bears traces of Spanish grille work in its design.

Aside from the white stitching detail on the black leather sofas, the rest of the interior is simple and contemporary, with oak and black leather furniture, polished Cascais stone floors and towering windows lined by large oak louvers to shield the interior from the strong Spanish sun. Lighting elements introduce more intimate, human proportions, with large white pendant lamps extending from the soaring ceiling down the centre of the room, and smaller lamps, hung by red cords, suspended over each table.

Philippe Starck's first Moscow restaurant is a macabre affair. He was persuaded to create a third Bon in the Russian capital by the owners of the Billionaire Club (the original Bon and its sequel, Bon 2, are both in Paris). Apparently Starck was not a fan of Moscow, but he nevertheless agreed to create the 140-seat Italian restaurant in a nineteenth-century building (neighbouring the club) in Yakimanskaya Quay. It opened in April 2006 and the result is a flamboyantly noir interior that celebrates 'the New Russian trinity of sex, violence and food' (www.yankodesign.com, June 2006).

Starck's chaotic blend of gold and black bespoke pieces – imposing stained-glass windows of strange man-beast creations, candelabra dripping with wax and black crystal chandeliers – with salvaged trophies and curios of stuffed owls and skulls conjures up a hauntingly gothic atmosphere. Lighting levels are low, with black lamps of varying heights complementing flickering candlelight; most spectacular are those supported by gleaming golden Kalashnikov bases. Furniture includes half-burned gilded armchairs and dining couches upholstered in black fabric emblazoned with white embroidered skulls – also a popular motif on the catwalk in 2006. All this is set against a backdrop of risqué frescos and distressed walls defaced with unsettling, violently scrawled graffiti.

Uncanny though the setting may seem, when it comes to fashion and interiors all things black, and often with a hint of morbidity, are very much in vogue – as proven by the many stylish Moscovites who are flocking to dine in this ghoulish lair.

Over the last few years pattern has made a huge comeback in commercial interiors, whether in the form of wall coverings, fabric, etched and layered glass detailing or clever laser-cut metals and plastics. Tangentially there has also been a move towards pared-down colour schemes; contrasting monochrome has made a comeback, and all-black or all-white interiors are also popular – the latter particularly so in hot countries with an abundance of bright sunlight.

The Italian restaurant Isola, completed by Leigh & Orange in May 2004, is a prime example of both these trends. A new build, the 650 square metre (7,000 square foot) restaurant and bar is located on levels three and four of the International Finance Centre, overlooking the glittering harbour in Hong Kong's Central district. In keeping with the honest Italian food rustled up in the copper-walled open kitchen, project designer Hugh Zimmern has kept things simple in the restaurant, combining rustic oak with immaculate white furniture.

The entrance is rural in style, with tall, stable-like concertina doors of oak pushed open to reveal oak floors and timber wine storage. There are few extraneous extras, although a small private dining room is partially screened off by a curved metal grid strung with silver kitchen utensils, beaten flat to appear almost two-dimensional. This fun, rather utilitarian form of decoration has captured the

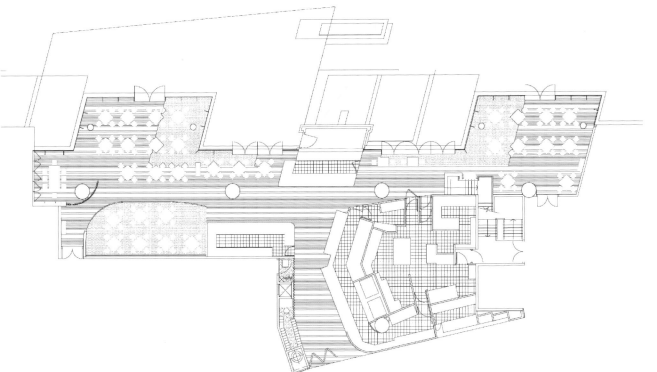

FAR LEFT
Lace-like metalwork decorates the dining room at Isola.

ABOVE
Towering rustic oak doors mark the entrance.

LEFT
Plan: the 650 square metre (7,000 square foot) restaurant and bar seats a total of 300 patrons.

zeitgeist, too. In an aesthetic bid to return to honesty, restaurant designers across the world are often displaying grocery items and kitchen wares as decoration.

At Isola the elegance and sophistication is provided by the incredibly intricate, lace-like walls and ceiling of the dining area. Designed by Lilian Tang, this decorative layer is composed of a 3mm (⅛ inch) thick, hard metal plate, perforated to create a complex pattern of flora and fauna. Laid against white walls, the pattern is part of an inter-play of light and shadow created by sunlight that floods in through the floor-to-ceiling windows. The effect is like delicately textured lace upon linen. Tang's design is repeated in bas relief on the curved white-washed concrete block wall at the entrance.

Isola is a fine example of how even in a monochrome setting pattern can bring texture and visual stimulation.

LEFT
A private dining area is sectioned off by a metal screen strung with beaten kitchen utensils.

RIGHT
Isola's distinctive lacework pattern is repeated in bas-relief form on the white-washed concrete façade.

PREVIOUS PAGE
Amsterdammers love the communal dining available at the central banqueting tables at Mansion.

THIS PAGE

LEFT
Ground-floor plan showing the Sistine Chapel carpet design in the Black Bar (right).

BELOW LEFT
Plan of the first-floor restaurant with its three interconnecting rooms.

TOP RIGHT
Concrete's contemporary mirrored cornicing gives everything a silver lining in the Cocktail Bar.

BOTTOM RIGHT
Monroe and Sinatra add glamour to The Mansion's entrance corridor.

Concrete is best known as the creator of Amsterdam's influential Supperclub concept, where guests dine communally, reclining against white pillows on giant white bunk beds. There are now Supperclubs in Rome, San Francisco and Istanbul. In its native city of Amsterdam, Concrete is responsible for many other restaurant projects including Blender, Nomads and Envy. In 2005 it completed The Mansion. The brief was to create a contemporary gentleman's-club-meets-modern-nightlife-establishment in a grand, historic three-storey property that had previously housed the Michelin-star restaurant Vossius. 'It was a very old villa and we thought we would bring it back but in a modern way, so it was still baroque but had a modern twist to it,' says Concrete founder Rob Wagemans.

Maintaining the existing layout, Concrete divided the property into several areas, forming different environments. Three cocktail bars (The Cocktail Bar, Black Bar and Rosé Room) are on the ground floor, the restaurant is on the first floor and the funkier Dim Sum club occupies the basement. Modern design interpretations of the building's heritage features provide unifying motifs that retain a sense of aesthetic cohesion throughout. These include the framing of doorways, bars, furniture and walls with a contemporary, mirrored interpretation of classic cornicing, giving everything a glamorous silver-edging that imparts a sense of bygone decadence. Walls throughout are covered with a classic pattern in a modern material: vinyl wallpaper with a relief of Viscaya lilies is paired with delicate chrome wall-lights that have colour co-ordinated shades to complement the palette of each particular room.

The light, silvery-white entrance is composed of brushed stainless-steel flooring cut to resemble herringbone parquet, silver walls, alcoves housing mirrors and mirrored cornicing. By contrast, the first-floor dining rooms are a dramatically dark, regal shade of purple paired with gunmetal grey. These are probably the most classic rooms of all due to their listed nature, so rather than make any radical design statements, Concrete has enhanced their inherent grandeur to create an opulent dining experience. Decorative existing ceilings and mantelpieces, topped by gilt-framed mirrors, are painted off-white, and windows are dressed with delicate purple lace curtains flanked by purple velour drapes. A smoked oak parquet floor is partially covered by a purple rug.

The two adjourning dining rooms and salon privé are dominated by 4 metre (13 foot) long, banqueting style tables that seat 12 diners. Constructed from stained timber, the tables feature synthetic mirrored cornice edges and ornate, reflective table tops composed of purple synthetic mirror bearing a sheet of glass engraved with the Viscaya lily pattern of the grey wallpaper. Silver and crystal chandeliers suspended above, and reflected by, these table tops further maximize the sense of grandeur.

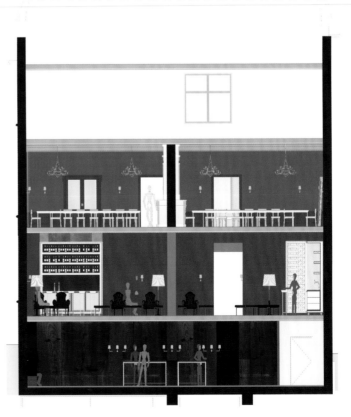

The banqueting tables have proved very popular with people specifically booking to sit there. Concrete is a big advocate of communal dining – as Wagemans says: 'Social life in Amsterdam is easier than the rest of Holland, people like sitting with strangers and are curious to see what kind of neighbours they're going to have. It's socializing in an unexpected way, not quite like a dating service, but you can meet other people and join in to other people's discussions. It's something we really like.'

Smaller tables are similarly finished and, in keeping with the classic silver theme, are paired with glossy polished aluminium chairs – Gervasoni's InOut 23 by Paola Navone. A small adjoining lounge features a contrasting lighter palette. Low, chrome-legged benches lining the walls are upholstered in imitation ostrich leather and tiny chrome-framed pedestal tables with white 'Vanilla' Corian tops are edged by the ubiquitous synthetic mirror cornice detail.

Downstairs the three bars are full of statement pieces, from the Cocktail Bar's chrome, steel and mirror bar units – designed to resemble super-sized, old-fashioned drinks cabinets and lit by LEDs to form a golden glowing presence – to the Black Bar's illuminated fabric ceiling and matching carpet displaying a modern take on the Sistine chapel ceiling. 'That's what is so great about modern technology,' says Wagemans. 'The Sistine Chapel in Rome took Michelangelo 11 years to paint, but it took us one and half hours to print.' Nothing, it seems, is too grand for The Mansion.

FAR LEFT, TOP
The mirrored Cocktail Bar is modelled on an open drinks cabinet.

FAR LEFT, BOTTOM
Sections showing, from bottom, the basement club, ground-floor bars and first-floor restaurant.

LEFT
In the Black Bar drinkers sip cocktails surrounded by images of Michelangelo's Sistine Chapel masterpiece.

BISTRO & EL MERCADO

BUENOS AIRES ARGENTINA PHILIPPE STARCK

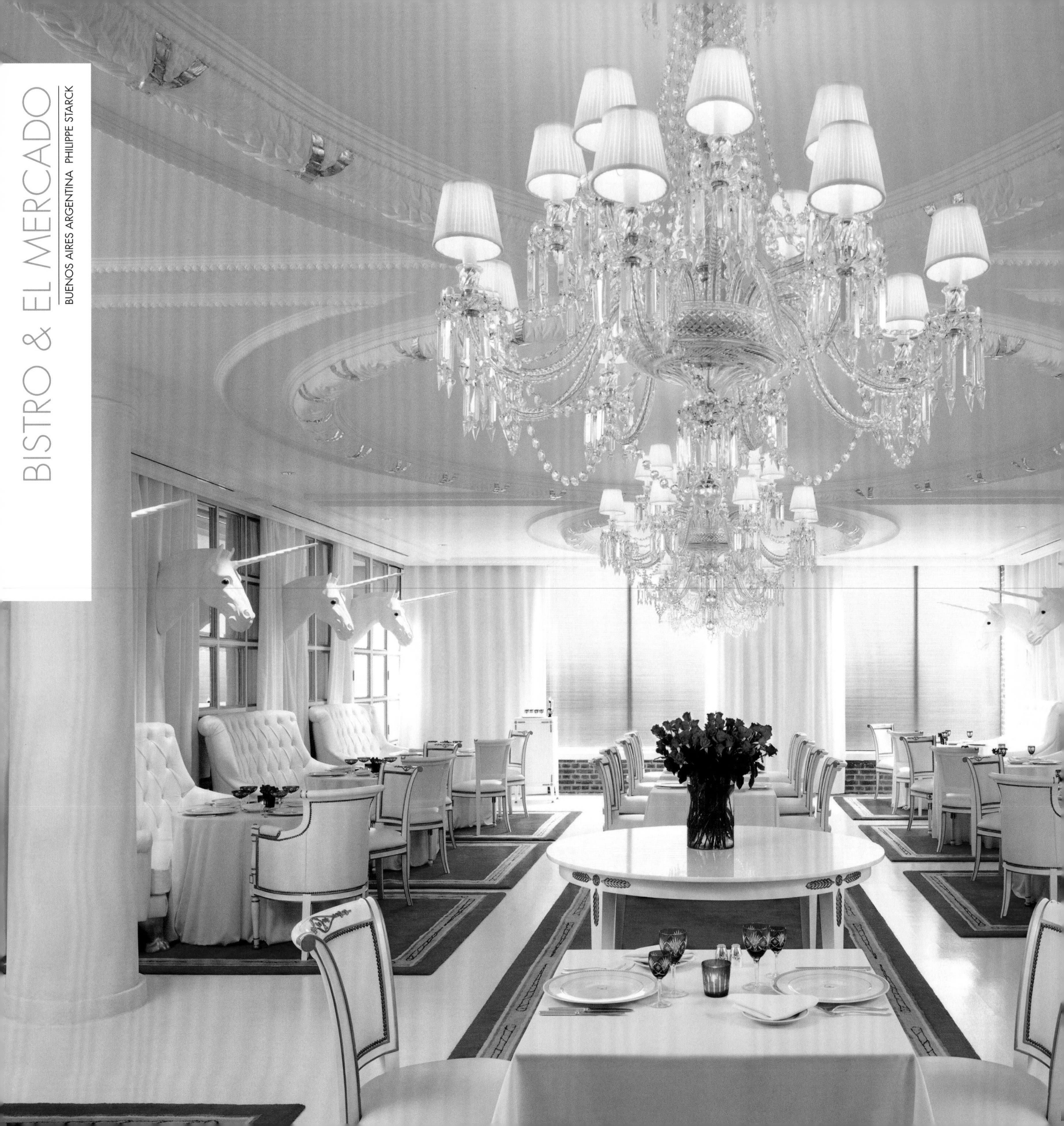

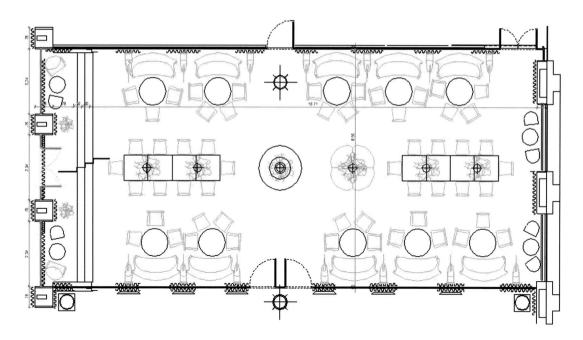

ABOVE
Plan of Bistro, where
symmetry provides a
sense of classical
elegance.

LEFT
Unicorns are the
perfect mythological
beast to complement
Starck's white-and-
scarlet fantasy.

The rather ostentatiously titled Faena Hotel + Universe, a $100 million collaboration between Buenos Aires entrepreneur and fashion designer Alan Faena and Philippe Starck, has been credited with injecting the Argentinean capital with a serious dose of cosmopolitan cool ever since it opened in 2005. According to the international style press, Faena Hotel + Universe is – like most Starck-designed hotels – where the city's beautiful people and creative crème de la crème congregate. Starck's lavish crimson, white and gilt interior pays extravagant homage to Buenos Aires's Belle Epoque heyday. How fitting that this French-born designer should be involved in the city's noughties renaissance, since back in the 1890s it was dubbed the 'Paris of South America', due to the strong influence of the French capital upon its architecture and cultural life.

Starck and Faena's opulent creation occupies an historical landmark property in the regenerated dock area of Puerto Madero. A redbrick, former grain warehouse known as the El Porteño building, which dates back to 1902, now houses Faena's seven-storey, 105-bedroom 'universe'. Amongst the various five-star attractions (spa, hammam, cabaret, pool and so on) comprising the ground floor, Starck has created two contrasting restaurants: the Bistro, serving international gourmet food, and El Mercado, furnished with a wood-burning oven and producing more regional dishes.

The Bistro fine-dining salon is pure fairytale fantasy – a vision in white befitting the *Wizard of Oz*, or some such dreamscape. Elegant snow-white furniture is given a regal edge with classical gilt detailing, unicorn heads protrude from walls dressed in white silk, while the mythical unicorn horn motif is repeated in the simple border design of

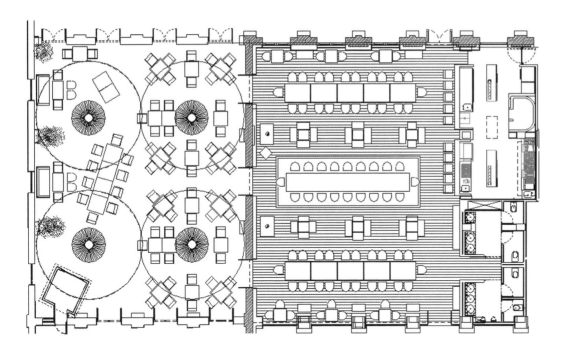

ABOVE
Plan of El Mercado: the
communal table is a
signature Starck element.

RIGHT
Hardwood floors and
brick walls lend El
Mercado a rustic feel.

crimson rugs below. Red Baccarat crystal and gold-rimmed plates complete the scene. Although this is clearly a Starck production that could operate anywhere in the world, the decorative moulded ceiling and mammoth crystal chandeliers were apparently inspired by the grand cafés and great patisseries of Buenos Aires from the early 1900s such as La Ideal and Café Tortoni. Such details celebrate a time when Argentina was a world power and cultural centre.

El Mercado, with its scrubbed hardwood flooring, exposed brick walls and discreet lighting, is far more rustic and authentic in feel, although it is still discernibly Starck with its fancy gold-leafed imperial-style chairs, long communal banqueting tables and glass display cases full of curiosities and antiques (albeit sourced locally from San Telmo). As the name suggests, it was 'inspired by old European markets and mythic cantinas', hence the outdoor terrace, which includes a fresh food market where local merchants sell their wares. Inside, the Belle Epoque lives on in the glass cabinets displaying antique china, silver and glassware and in the aluminium-tiled ceiling that was salvaged from original buildings of that glamorous bygone era. And finally, just to confirm El Mercado's Latin pedigree, the walls are decorated with photographs and portraits of famous Argentineans from Eva Perón to Diego Maradona.

COSPAIA

BRUSSELS BELGIUM WOLTERINCK

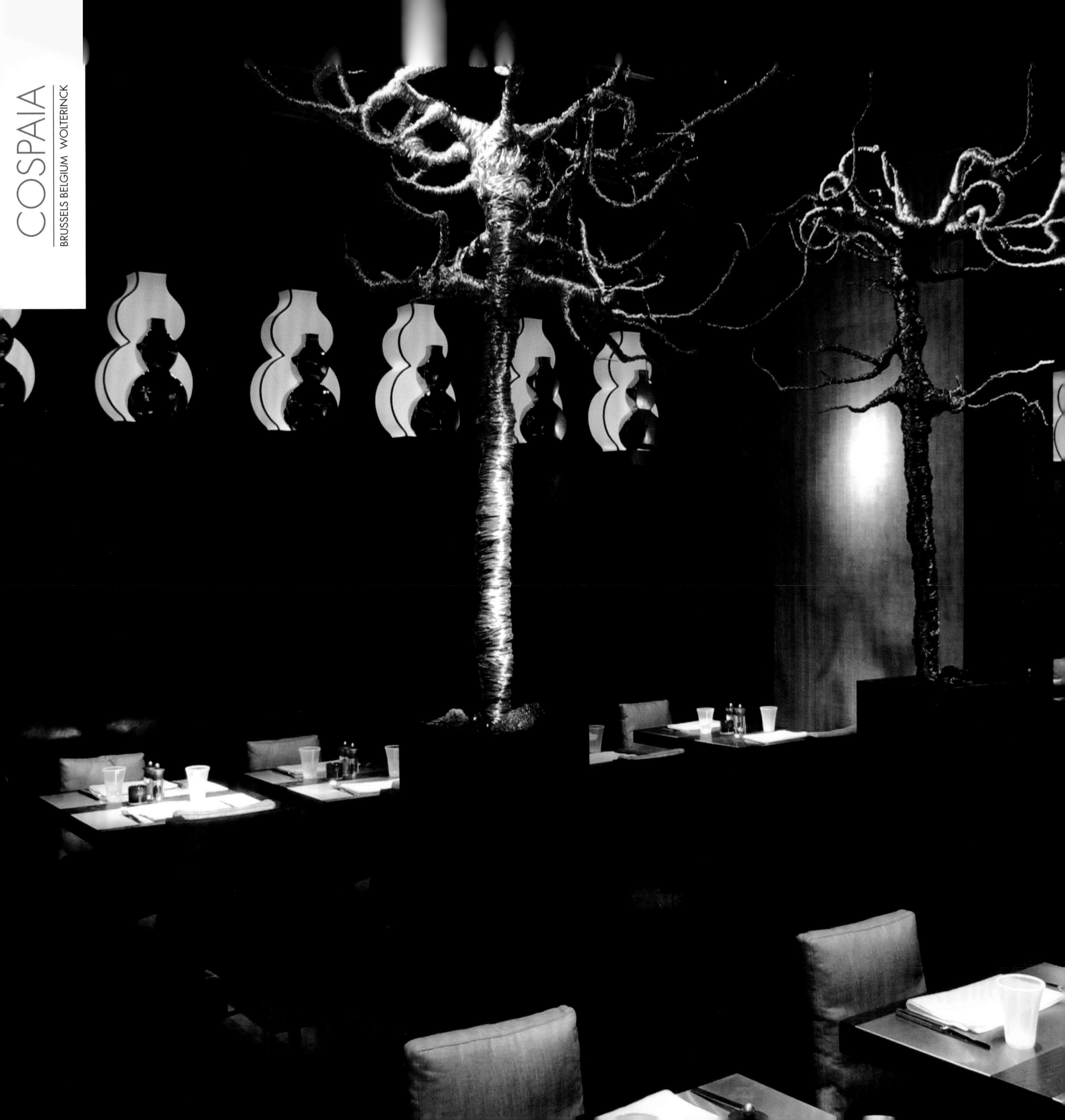

LEFT
Wolterinck's
tree sculptures
are spun from
silver wire.

ABOVE
Sketch of the
restaurant's
landscaped
entrance.

RIGHT
Dark stairs
are lined by
a textured
leather wall.

Dutch interior designer Marcel Wolterinck began his career as a florist, opening a florist shop in Laren in 1986. Over the past 20 years he has branched out into 'lifestyle decorating' – Cospaia is his first restaurant project. The restaurant and bar, overseen by top Belgian chef Jean-Pierre Bruneau, is located on Brussels' exclusive Boulevard de la Toison d'Or, close to designer fashion boutiques and five-star hotels. Owner Jan Tindemans chose the historic listed property for its character and address: 'I fell in love with the building: the beautiful ceilings, the baroque inspired rooms and the fantastic 180 square metre (1,939 square foot) terrace with a view of the lively boulevard de Waterloo.'

Story has it that Wolterinck camped for a week in the empty property 'to get inspired by the atmosphere'. The result is a study in monochrome. The listed historic 'baroque' dining room is painted white, in stark contrast to the remainder of Cospaia, which is predominantly black with silver accents. Like all the best restaurants, the entrance hints tantalizingly at the interior beyond, with a moody, minimal staircase of stone-grey marble finished with a black steel rail. This is softened by a textured wall covering composed of horizontal strips of leather, which also counterbalances the steep vertical of the stairwell.

The first floor of Cospaia comprises a bar, lounge and two dining rooms, accommodating 170 diners in total. Wolterinck's intention was to create a 'mysterious atmosphere', as guests arrive first in a rather noir bar area furnished with two heavy, communal high tables of black brushed oak paired with brown leather bar stools with stainless steel bases. A black, brushed-oak bar is topped by aubergine marble while the lower section of its façade is finished with dark-grey mirror to achieve a reflective, floating-above-the-floor effect.

Beyond the bar is a cosier lounge area, consisting of two bespoke seating systems; one C-shaped and the other oval. Continuing the sombre palette, tables are black oak and upholstery is in muted neutrals. A central floral display – top-lit by a custom-designed, aubergine-hued crystal chandelier – provides the focal point of the room.

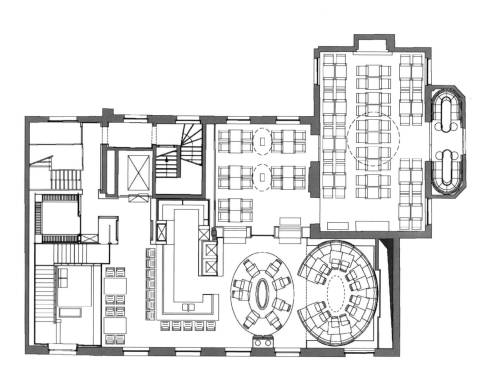

The adjacent 'silver' dining room is similarly dark but warmed by deep plum walls of 'tadelakt', a glossy textured lime plaster more typically used in the hammams and riads of Morocco. The room is lent an eerie air by two large silver organic sculptures – bare trees spun from iron wire by Wolterinck's atelier – dramatically lit by spotlights. Tables of black oak feature stainless-steel placemats and high-backed black chairs are furnished with silver cushions. Additional decoration is provided by a frieze of plinths, each supporting a voluptuous silver vase thrown into stark relief by a larger matching lamp positioned symmetrically behind.

The 'baroque' room is the tonal antithesis to this, with ornate, pure white tables dressed in white linen and 1940s style armchairs in white and plum. High ceilings lend a palatial feel, maximized by towering displays of verdant foliage in over-sized white vases. Wolterinck's sense of mystery is represented here in the form of six huge portraits, depicting the scarf-covered faces of Saharan Tuareg people, taken by French photographer Philippe Bourseiller.

ABOVE
Plan showing the two dining rooms (top right) and the lounge-bar areas with oval seating systems (bottom right).

RIGHT
Philippe Bourseiller's portraits of veiled Tuareg people complement Wolterinck's 'sense of mystery'.

Manhattan's Meatpacking district has developed into a buzzing destination neighbourhood at a remarkable rate, with designer boutiques and restaurants springing up alongside the few remaining meat wholesale companies that still operate there. Where once there were 250 such slaughterhouses and meatpacking plants, now there are fashion stores, private members' clubs, designer hotels and stylish restaurants such as Keith McNally's Pastis and Jean-Georges Vongerichten's Spice Market (see pages 26–7). The lofty industrial warehouses allow designers to create restaurants on an impressive scale. Christian Liaigre's Buddakan, which opened in March 2006 in a former Nabisco cookie factory, is one such recent arrival to the area.

Buddakan, a Modern Asian restaurant, is the New York sequel to its Philadelphia namesake; both are part of restaurateur Stephen Starr's burgeoning empire. In Philadelphia Starr has blazed a trail with his Starr Restaurant Organization, creating

über-hip venues by commissioning stellar designers such as David Schefer Design (Jones, Tangerine), David Rockwell (Pod, El Vez) and Karim Rashid (Morimoto).

Buddakan – and the nearby Morimoto by architect Tadao Ando – are Starr's first forays into New York. The former is a far more successful space, blending Asian detailing with a palatial, French Rococo grandeur to spectacular effect. Liaigre has called it 'a Versailles for New York' (*Interior Design*, January 2006), while Gerardo Olvera of lighting designers Isometrix describes it as 'French eighteenth-century decoration meets traditional Chinese style.' (*DDI* magazine, August 2006).

Reputed to have cost around $14 million, the bi-level Buddakan is a vast 1,486 square metre (16,000 square foot) restaurant accommodating up to 320 diners. Originally earmarked for the Buddha-Bar, a rudimentary structure was already in place when

LEFT
A sign of Bacchanalian things to come – the reception is decorated by a distressed reproduction of *The Feast of Acheloüs*.

ABOVE
Guests can gaze down into the main dining hall from the bar and mezzanine dining area.

FAR LEFT
Views up to the mezzanine from the 24-seat communal table.

LEFT
Dragons swoop down from the bespoke oak chandeliers.

RIGHT
Old-world grandeur reigns in the dramatic banqueting hall at the centre of Buddakan.

Liaigre took on the project, with the ground floor area elevated by 60 centimetres (two feet) to increase the height of the basement. It is this voluminous space that forms the dramatic centrepiece of Buddakan. Diners ascend several steps from street level into a lounge that leads into a dining mezzanine overlooking the soaring subterranean double-height banqueting hall.

Liaigre is a master of intensifying that sense of anticipation, and his entrances are always enigmatic, designed to tempt patrons inside. At Buddakan, the simple stainless-steel reception desk is dwarfed by a vast vinyl wall-hanging depicting a magnified version of the 1615 painting *The Feast of Acheloüs* by Peter Paul Rubens and Jan Brueghel the Elder. Distressed to appear antique, this hanging, which, combined with the towering brushed-oak panels opposite marking the entrance to the lounge, is a hint of both the sheer scale of the interior and the rarefied baroque aesthetic within.

The slightly austere lounge is typical of Liaigre's oeuvre – the neutral tones of the original

exposed brick, the grey granite floor and the furniture are brightened by strong accents of vibrant turquoise and yellow in the leather upholstery, the velvet brocade of the banquettes, lampshades and lacquered aluminium Asian-style fretwork screens that decorate the 'windows' overlooking the main hall. Muted versions of these hues appear in the landscape oil painting depicting seventeenth-century China that hangs above the stainless-steel bar. The remainder of the gallery mezzanine is devoted to dining, with timber flooring and bright orange and red lacquered screens creating a warmer mood, enhanced further by the glow of the colossal oak chandeliers and general hubbub of the diners in the great hall below.

Descent from the gallery into the theatrical dining hall is provided by a twin staircase of granite with a smoked glass balustrade. This soaring space, clad in $800,000 of blonde oak French-style boiserie is dominated by four giant oak chandeliers sporting dragons suspended above a central 9-metre (30-foot) long banqueting table. Angled spotlights above, orchestrated by

ABOVE
Vase-shaped apertures
frame doorways into the
Red Vase Room.

RIGHT
One of several dining
chambers leading off the
central hall.

FAR RIGHT
Golden books set the
Library aglow.

Isometrix, provide an additional design dimension, casting dramatic shadows across the oak walls and floor. Additional seating is provided by richly patterned banquettes lining the walls paired with high-backed chairs; all tables are topped by decorative bird-shaped candelabra.

Several smaller dining chambers lead off this central hall. The most dramatic is the Golden Library, its walls lined by white lacquered bookcases filled with rows of gilt-spined faux books, up- and down-lit to radiate a flatteringly warm glow. Elsewhere, in another perimeter dining area, walls are decorated by photographic portraits of Thai and Burmese Buddhas, some backlit and framed within a black lacquered grid. At the rear of the hall the Red Vase Room, furnished with two gargantuan glossy vases and red floral upholstered seating, is accessible via black timber-framed Oriental-shaped apertures set into a simple brick wall.

LEFT
The main dining space is partially illuminated by custom-designed sea urchin light fixtures.

ABOVE LEFT
Vintage pieces, such as this 1930s French commode, lend the space a regal air.

ABOVE RIGHT
Powder blue is used throughout – in the leather-upholstered chairs, wallpaper and curtains – to unite the space.

Los Angeles-based designer Kelly Wearstler is best known for her interiors for the Kor Hotel Group – predominantly West Coast properties including Avalon and Maison 140 in Beverly Hills, the Viceroy in Santa Monica and recently, on the east coast, Tides in Miami's South Beach. Since establishing Kelly Wearstler Interior Design (kwid) in the early 1990s, she has earned a reputation for creating sophisticated, glamorous hotel, retail and residential interiors awash with high-quality finishes and elegant detailing – a style she describes as 'old world Hollywood with a modern vibe'. Wearstler transposed some of this refined decadence to New York when she was asked to create a restaurant for Bergdorf Goodman, the exclusive department store on Manhattan's Fifth Avenue.

Originally built in 1928, Bergdorf Goodman lacked a formal restaurant until the 95-seat BG opened in November 2005. Wearstler was granted 185 square metres (2,000 square feet) on the seventh floor to produce 'a relaxed setting where people would feel comfortable having lunch three times a week, a space that was not gender specific and where anyone from age 20 to 80 would feel comfortable'. Located in the Decorative Home department,

the site previously housed three distinct shops. Wearstler drew upon her love of Paris, particularly its vintage and antique furniture, to transform these shops into a series of interconnecting salons with a distinctly Parisian feel.

The light colour palette, bleached oak floors, mirrored panels and silver leaf finishes enhance the fresh, daytime feel of BG, which closes by 8pm at the latest. Bespoke white wall panelling, featuring a diamond pattern outlined in black and gold leaf, lends the lounge bar, which precedes the main dining space, a regal air. This is enhanced by vintage pieces such as the French 1930s black-lacquered commodes, the chairs and sofas modelled on Deco designs, and the bronze tables. Golden leather canopy armchairs sit in pairs by the windows overlooking Central Park: 'They're like cocoons, so you don't feel too out in the open,' said Wearstler in *Interior Design* (April 2006).

Crowning the lounge is a custom-designed 'sea urchin' light fixture set within an octagonal ceiling cove. These fixtures also star in the main dining room, providing a sense of continuity throughout. Additional lounge lighting is provided

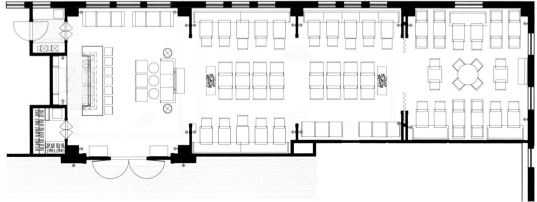

by Deco-style 'Sirenas' sconces, featuring shades supported by small mermaid figurines. Two French 1960s paintings, mounted back to back, form a screen marking the threshold between the lounge and dining room.

The main dining salon is a genteel affair furnished with a variety of chairs, powder-blue banquettes, distressed, antique-mirrored waiter stations, and De Gournay chinoiserie wallpaper in a delicate shade of robin's egg blue. Blue silk curtains can be drawn to separate a *salon privé* from the smaller dining chamber at the far end. This 32-seat room is warmer in feel. Shades of yellow dominate, with 'Sunview' leather seat pads on the lattice-backed chairs and gold and black appearing in the carpet and antique-mirrored wall panelling. There are also ivory wing-backed arm chairs embroidered with the distinctive BG logo, which was also designed by kwid, and which is echoed elsewhere in the octagonal shapes of the ceiling coves and panelling.

Bergdorf's senior vice president, Linda Fargo, described the finished project as 'part 1940s Park Avenue, part Hollywood Regency'. However you describe it, BG is surely refined enough to seduce even the most jaded of Bergdorf Blondes or Park Avenue Princesses.

FAR LEFT
The lounge bar features white panelling picked out with black and gold.

CENTRE LEFT
Ivory wing chairs bear the specially designed BG logo.

LEFT
1960s French paintings form a screen between the lounge and the dining room.

BELOW CENTRE
Plan, with the lounge bar to the left and the salon privé to the right.

BOTTOM
Sketch of the salon privé.

RIGHT
The chinoiserie wallpaper by De Gournary echoes the shades of blue, green and yellow used throughout.

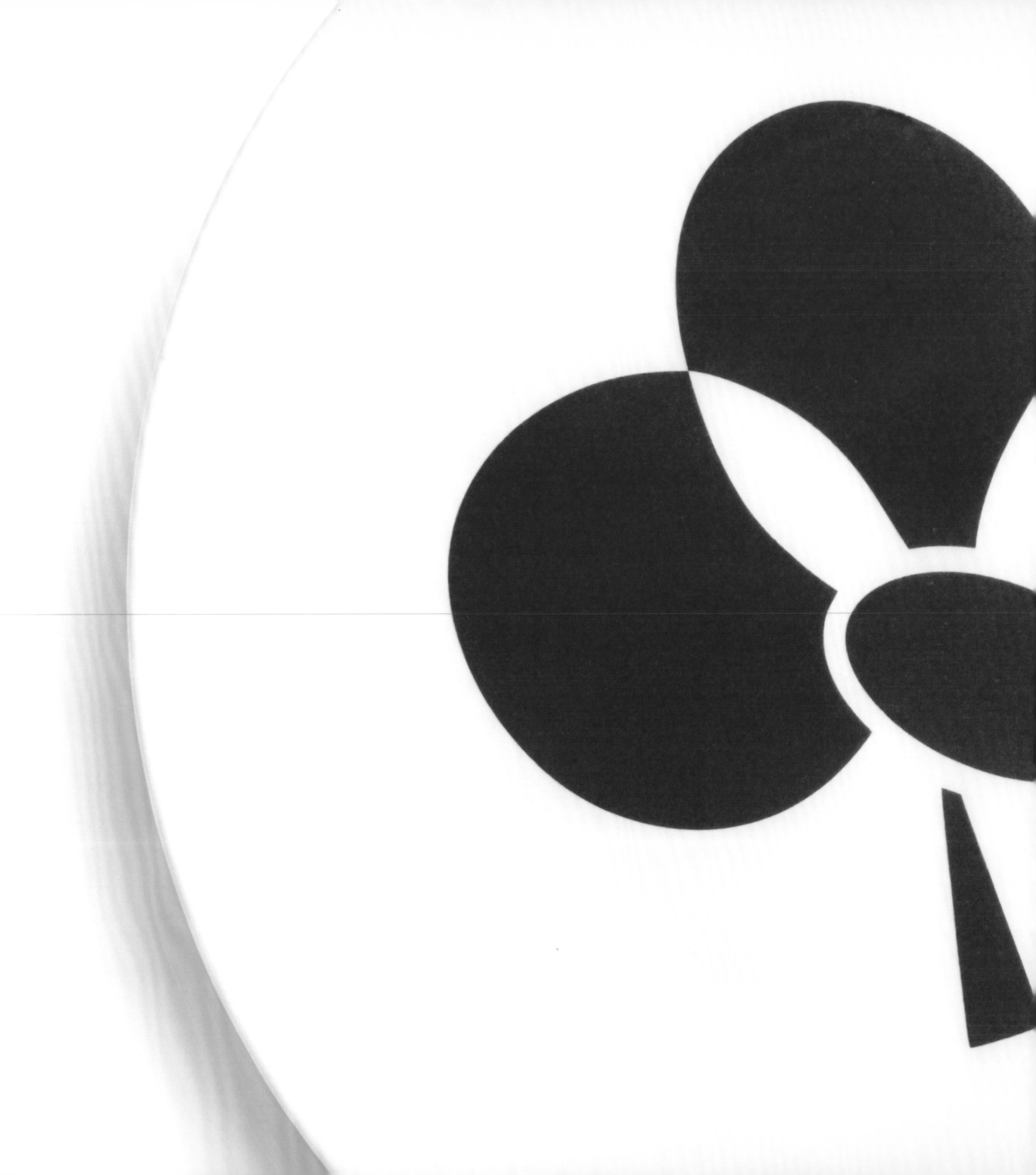

It's a brave and confident architect who undertakes a commission to design a restaurant interior in a new iconic Frank Gehry creation. However, Hagy Belzberg and his multiple award-winning Santa Monica-based team rose to the challenge after winning the competition to design the restaurant and retail space within the new Walt Disney Concert Hall in the Arts District of downtown Los Angeles. What's more, their novel response references Gehry's fluid, organic idiom while possessing a distinctive style of its own, as Belzberg intended. Determined that the interior wouldn't be overshadowed by Gehry's scene-stealing exterior, Belzberg said, 'We wanted to be respectful, but we had to have our own identity,' (*Architectural Record*, December 2003).

At first glance the restaurant, which was completed in October 2003, appears to follow clean, modernist lines, but a closer look reveals a deeper complexity. Inspired by the host building, Belzberg developed a design concept based on the allusion of a theatrical curtain. The initial idea – a stage curtain frozen in motion to reveal rippling folds – evolved into a three-dimensional format through a computer-aided design process. Form-Z software enabled Belzberg to create digital models of the sculptural forms and then transmit them to a milling machine to produce actual timber panels from huge, solid 362 kilo (800 pound) blocks of laminated walnut (measuring 0.9–1.2 metres by 2.4 metres/3–4 feet by 8 feet). These clear varnished panels were then attached to the walls of the restaurant using steel angles and ledgers.

The result is both texturally and tonally enriching, with large walnut panels hanging like rippling silk around the walls of the restaurant. Belzberg writes: 'The superimposition of ruled wood grain with fluctuating surface pattern registers as a curtain drawn around the perimeter of the dining room. The activity and ambience of the restaurant is held behind the fluid enclosure as a kind of "behind-the-scenes" post-performance experience.' Architecture critic Joseph Giovannini summarizes the effect in relation to the expressionist forms of the host structure: 'Translating billowy "sails" into wavy "fabric", the panels restate Gehry's larger gestures in miniature. Abstractly, Belzberg reduced to a decorative scale the turbulent forms rolling through Gehry's building.' (*Architectural Record*, as before).

Meanwhile, the ceiling follows a similar theme with a gently contoured, undulating surface composed of plywood strips. Golden yellow light radiates from cold-cathode lighting wrapped in copper film, which is contained within the grooves between the strips, adding warmth to the interior.

Not only did Gehry approve of the design, but Belzberg won the AIA Restaurant Design Award 2005 for the scheme, and chef Joachim Splichal's Mediterranean food is winning plaudits all round, making Patina as much a destination as the concert venue itself.

LEFT
Glass doors slide across to create a private dining salon.

ABOVE
Guests enter the bar first which is decorated by a wine display with bottles protruding from a back-lit translucent wall.

RIGHT
The 465 square metre (5,000 square feet) restaurant seats 112 inside and a further 48 on the patio. 1. entrance, 2. chef's table, 3. patio, 4. kitchen, 5. bar, 6. dining room, 7. private dining room, 8. toilets.

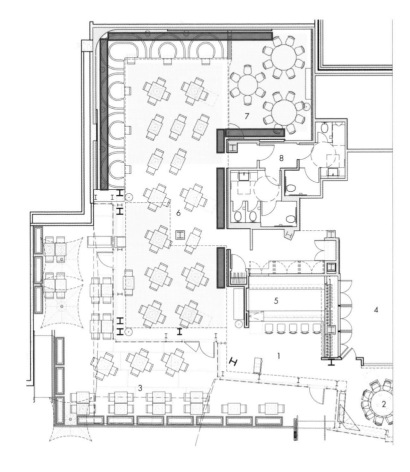

FASANO

SÃO PAULO BRAZIL ISAY WEINFELD

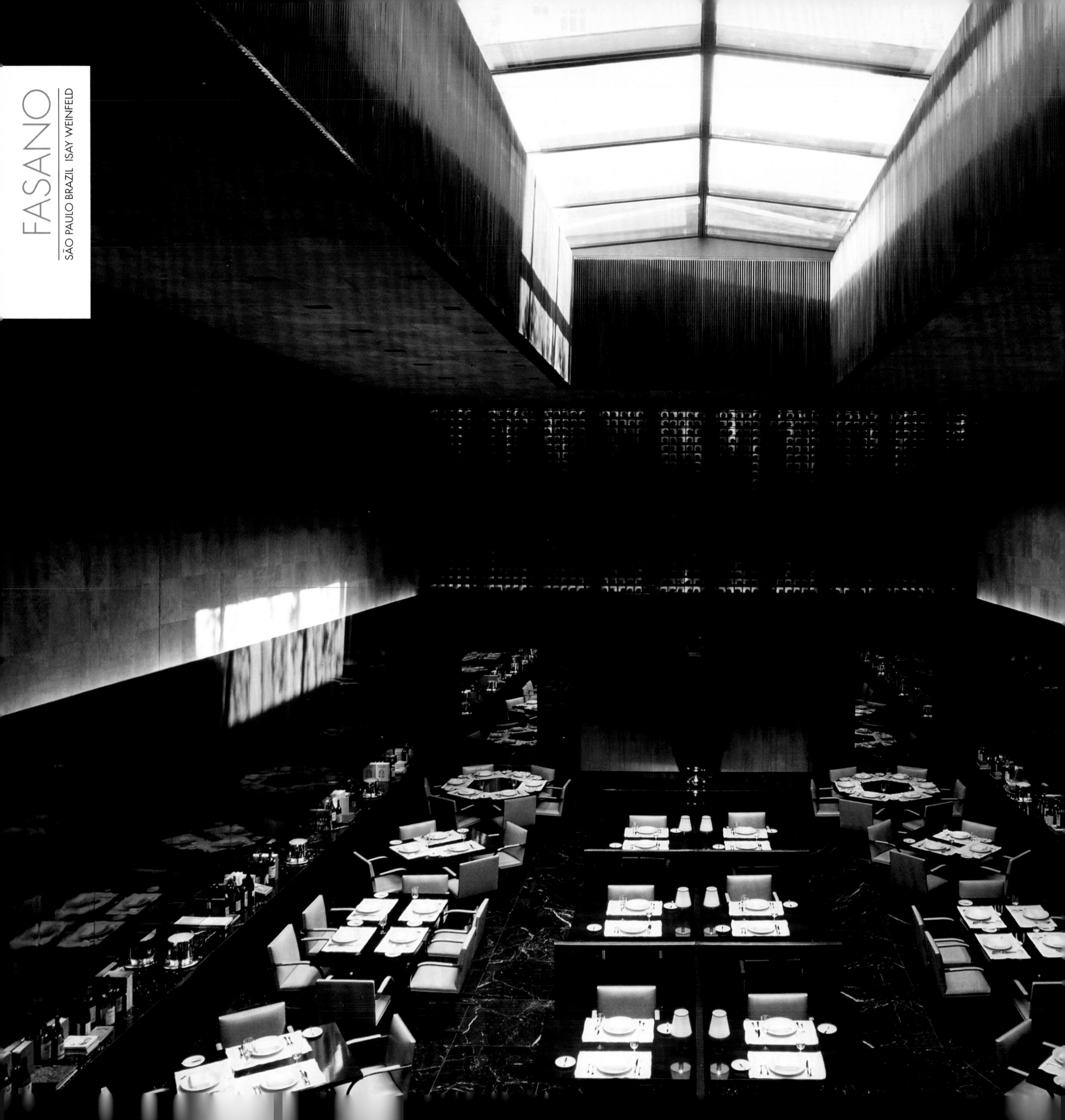

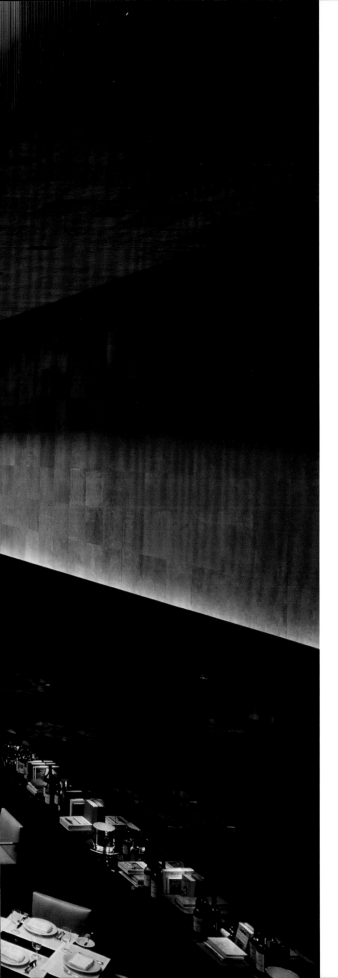

LEFT
A birds-eye
view from the
private dining
mezzanine.

ABOVE
Guests first enter
a small, moodily
lit bar that leads
through into
the restaurant.

São Paulo-based architect Isay Weinfeld is well known in Brazil for a wide variety of projects ranging from corporate buildings to residential villas, from restaurants to a boutique hotel. 'Tropical modernism' is the term critics have used to describe his particular style of architecture, which references mid-century modernism while employing the rich, native materials of Brazil. One of Weinfeld's longest standing clients is Rogério Fasano, for whom he has created several restaurants and cafés as well as the eponymous São Paulo boutique hotel and restaurant which opened in September 2003.

The Fasano Hotel and Restaurant is a new build located among the designer fashion stores in the leafy Jardins neighbourhood of the city. Weinfeld was asked to create a restaurant with a 'contemporary, elegant design'. The spacious interior is only accessible from the hotel lobby and comprises a small holding bar and 80-seat dining room on the ground floor, and private dining for 26 people on a mezzanine level; kitchens, storage and toilets are in the basement.

Employing an aesthetic very much akin to the 'international style' typified by Mies van der Rohe's Barcelona Pavilion, Weinfeld's talent is creating simple interiors that manage to appear incredibly rich and textured through a generous use of natural materials such as heavily grained woods and veined marbles. Fasano restaurant is a signature project, the grand proportions allowing Weinfeld to liberally indulge his spare palette. The result is a vision of honey, caramel and golden hues warmed by an abundance of natural light that pours down from an expansive retractable glass ceiling above.

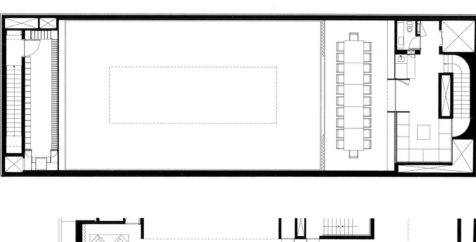

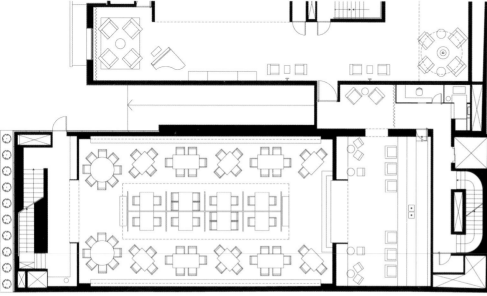

Guests arrive in the small 18-seat bar, which is moodily lit and compact in comparison to the airy dining room beyond, though it is furnished in similar materials – a bar countertop of Noir Saint Laurent marble, a woven cane screen ceiling and Florence Knoll swivel chairs. Diners depart the bar by descending a few steps into the restaurant.

The restaurant's lower walls are lined in glossy dark embuia timber, the reflective capacity of which maximizes the sense of space in the absence of windows. The upper walls and ceiling are lined in acoustically and visually softening suede panelling. Custom-designed

tables with oxidized bronze frames and embuia timber tops are paired with Mies van der Rohe's classic chrome and leather 'Brno' chairs. Floors of highly polished Noir Saint Laurent marble complete the mid-century modern feel.

Lighting is recessed or discreetly concealed within structural elements – such as the vast wine storage unit that fills the end wall. Occasional light is provided by the table lamps custom-designed by Weinfeld that illuminate the tables for two. These tables flank each side of the central woven cane and bronze-framed partition, creating a sense of intimacy in an otherwise open-plan space.

TOP LEFT
Plan of the mezzanine level with private dining room.

BOTTOM LEFT
Plan of the main level, with the bar to the right.

RIGHT
In the main dining room Mies van der Rohe chairs and polished marble floors lend a mid-century modern feel.

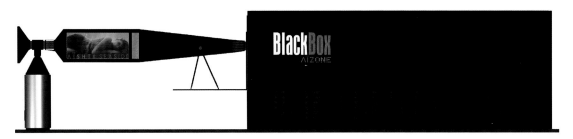

Lebanese architect Bernard Khoury (who has renamed his practice DW5) has, through his daring and creative reclamation of war-torn buildings, played a major role in Beirut's recent, much-reported renaissance. His militaristic, bunker-style club B018 remains an iconic symbol of the city's new found party spirit and his later restaurant projects Centrale, with a retractable roof over the bar, and the rocket-like Yabani proved that its cititzens were ready to embrace a new architecture and a sophisticated dining scene.

Black Box diner opened in July 2005 and is undeniably Khoury. Situated just outside the city on the northbound side of the Jal ed Dib highway, it is the neighbouring restaurant of Aïzone, a five-storey branch of the designer fashion department store Aïshti – Beirut's answer to Harvey Nichols or Barney's. The restaurant and store are part of a roadside row of Aïshti-owned properties that are decorated by various advertising billboards announcing the retailer. The original industrial building that was to become Black Box was set about 20 metres (65 feet) further back than the neighbouring façades, and so it was Khoury's aim to highlight its presence from the highway.

Black aluminium composite panels lining the exterior give the building strong definition. From this solid, somewhat austere façade Khoury projected an industrial structure that resembles some kind of military surveillance equipment. 'We created a steel "arm" that projects out from the front façade to catch up on the imposed setback and forcefully address the highway,' explains Khoury. Within the structure of the arm a large three-dimensional picture frame allows the display of images – and could even accommodate actual catwalk shows – produced by Aïshti. A 5 metre by 3 metre (16 foot by 10 foot) screen at the end of the arm provides another advertising opportunity, showing ads or images from special events. Incorporated into the steel cylinder that supports this arm is a cash machine: 'The assemblage of the installation recognizes and amplifies contemporary society's reliance on the trendiest fashions, latest entertainment venues and the facility of money distributors,' comments Khoury.

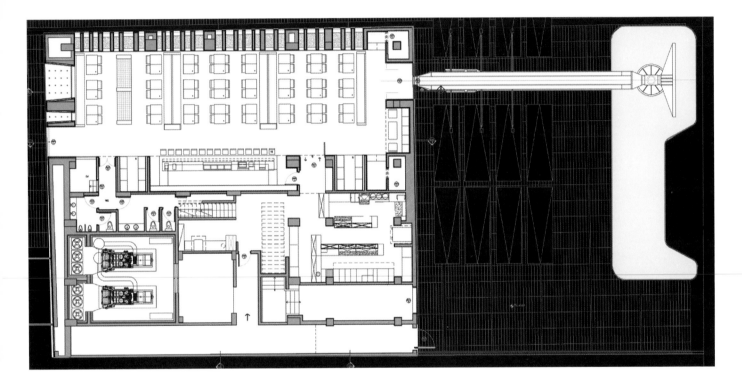

Inside, the central columns were removed and lighting recessed into the ceiling to create a clear, open-plan interior that allows diners views through to the sea beyond. The palette is simple, with custom-made furnishings in Aïshti's corporate colours of black and red, the latter enhancing the diner-like feel. Bar and table tops are – fittingly for a diner – black Formica, and chairs and banquettes constructed from MDF painted red with black, faux-leather seats. Khoury always creates the furniture for his projects and pieces often display a mid-century modern influence; at Black Box there are deep banquettes of button-studded black leather reminiscent of Mies van

der Rohe's furniture. In the north-facing, rear seaside elevation, Khoury has incorporated external recessed sofas in red, creating an alfresco area where guests can relax and admire the sea.

It is to be hoped that damage inflicted by the July 2006 conflict between Israel and Hezbollah is not irreversible, and that Beirut's confidence and hard-won cosmopolitan atmosphere will continue to flourish and, with it, a new architecture.

TOP LEFT
Alfresco seats at the rear allow guests to gaze out to sea.

TOP RIGHT
View through the diner-style restaurant to the sea beyond.

ABOVE
Plan: the interior includes a small bar (centre) and seats just over 100 diners (top). The advertising arm is to the right.

RIGHT
Central columns were removed to create a free-flowing open-plan space.

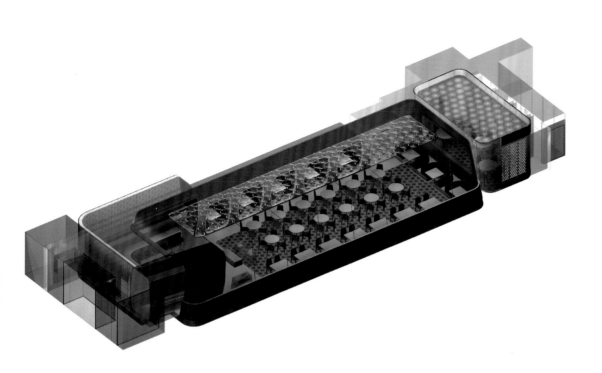

LEFT
Guests travel from the dark
reception through a bright
sloping hexagonal Corian
tunnel into the restaurant.

ABOVE
Computer-rendered model
of the layout with main
dining room in the centre
and the private salon at the
rear (to the right of the
model).

ABOVE RIGHT
Backlit mirrored-glass
featuring the hexagonal
motif provides the backdrop
to dining booths.

The ultimate venue for power dining in Manhattan has long been the Philip Johnson-designed Four Seasons restaurant in Mies van der Rohe's Seagram Building. But ever since August 2003 this dapper old gent has experienced serious competition in the form of a popular young upstart: a subterranean restaurant in the basement of the glassy Lever House on Park Avenue. Classed as a Modernist icon in 1983, Lever House was designed by Gordon Bunshaft of Skidmore, Owings and Merrill and built in 1952. The 21-storey building only ever had a cafeteria for employees, but the current leaseholders decided that part of a large-scale restoration project on the property should include a new destination restaurant.

A group of New York restaurateurs led by Joshua Pickard and John McDonald seized the opportunity of turning the 600 square metre (6,500 square foot) space, formerly a conference room, into a landmark restaurant that was 'special and unexpected' (Vanity Fair, September 2003). They commissioned Australian architect Marc Newson, who has applied his signature retro-futuristic aesthetic to everything from cars and aeroplanes to restaurants, bars and vibrators. There was no brief, simply a $5 million budget, and the project took 25 months from the initial design stage to completion.

Newson's design – based on a hexagonal shape and executed in materials and lighting that create a warm sunny yellow interior – has been aptly described as a 'honeycomb hideout' and 'power hive' (Vanity Fair, as before). Accentuating first impressions of the 154-cover restaurant is the black reception and lobby area in which guests arrive from 53rd street. This serves as a kind of sensual-deprivation antechamber, the blackness intensifying the experience of descending through the bright, 6 metre (20 foot) hexagonal tunnel of thermoformed cameo-white Corian into the glowing honeyed warmth of the restaurant.

Newson says: 'I was obsessed with honouring the building with a kind of decadent use of materials.' The walls and ceiling of the main dining room are finished in traditional Kyokabe plaster more typically found in the tea houses of Japan, combined with blonde, Victorian oak panelling. The geometric honeycomb motif is repeated throughout the scheme, from the custom-designed wool carpet and wine storage behind the bar, to the ceiling, which features 150 suspended hexagonal concrete elements hosting lights and services such as speakers and air-conditioning units. The bar stools and oak and leather chairs were custom-made for Lever House.

ABOVE
Booths are elevated by
15 centimetres (6 inches)
to encourage voyeuristic
behaviour.

RIGHT
Sliding glass panels
screen-off the 22-seat
salon privé.

A vital ingredient for any high-profile Manhattan restaurant seeking to attract the city's major players is the ample opportunity to see and be seen. Lever House Restaurant offers plenty of voyeuristic possibilities, not least in the row of slightly elevated booths lining one side of the room. Each booth is framed by a large, oak-lined hexagonal opening and set against an illuminated mirrored-glass backdrop, sandblasted with the recurring honeycomb motif.

The salon privé, located at the end of the room and framed by a large aperture fitted with sliding panes of glass, is, ironically, even more stage-like. Raised above the main dining room, the salon allows prime public viewing. A completely illuminated ceiling, which is composed of 70 translucent hexagonal elements made by Barrisol (each one hosting a torus light) makes the private dining room appear even more radiant than the rest of this power-dining honey pot.

FRISSON

SAN FRANCISCO USA KESTER INC/ARCHITECTURE TM

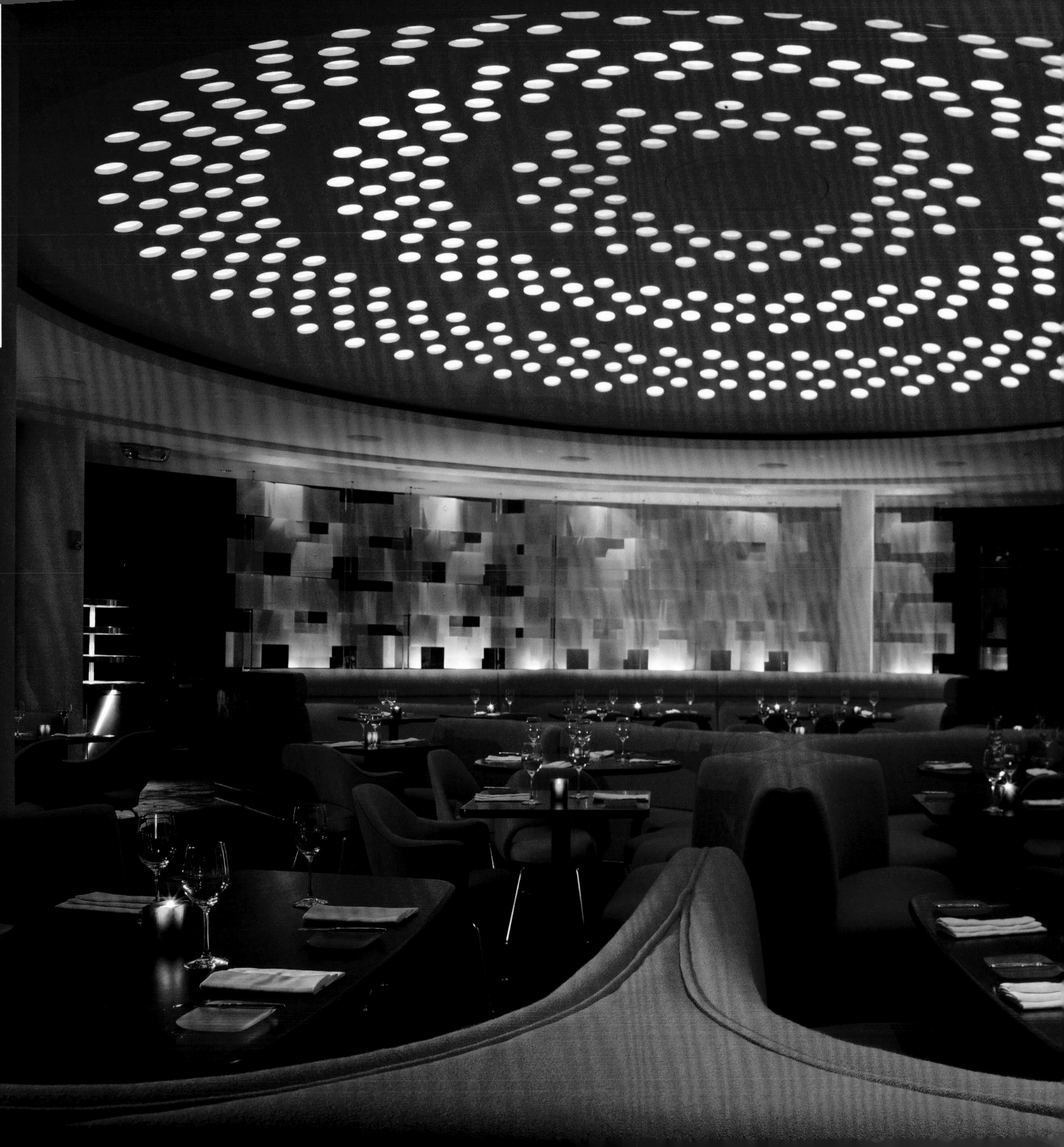

Supper clubs are very much in vogue and New York-based designer Scott Kester is a bit of an expert, having co-designed several such establishments in New York and Miami – Lotus and Rumi respectively – with Nancy Mah before forming his own practice in 2003. Frisson, created in collaboration with Architecture TM, is Kester Inc's first restaurant project. The budget was $5 million and it opened in August 2004.

Discussing inspiration for the project in *Interior Design* magazine (January 2005), Kester references a bygone era: 'Transatlantic ocean liners from the 1920s and 1930s have corridors opening onto a vast ballroom, this huge glamorous space where everything happens. There's a feeling of luxury associated with that, and Frisson stimulates that kind of fantasy.' He was also influenced by the 'modern retail design principles' of Morris Lapidus, America's godfather of curvy, kitsch and glamorous post-war architecture who created many of Miami's hotels, including the Fontainebleau.

Lapidus's design rules – use sweeping lines, create unusual effects with light for drama, change floor levels and keep people moving – are neatly embodied within Frisson's central attraction: a circular dining room crowned by a dome featuring a galaxy of lights. Kester explains: 'The circular dining room permits a continuous flow of service and customer circulation from the front to the back of space. Just like a ballroom dancefloor, there is an arena relationship between diners in the centre and those seated on the perimeter; observed and observing.'

The 94-seat supper club occupies the ground and basement floors of an office building erected in 1909. Guests enter through a long corridor, lined in brown vinyl, which leads directly into the warm sunset glow of the dining circle. The circle is defined by curved, modular banquettes and a series of mahogany-backed booths upholstered in an orange wool fabric. At the centre is a tripartite seating cluster with three large booths at the heart and off-shoots of banquette seating. Bespoke mahogany-topped tables and Eero Saarinen's 1957 'Executive' chairs, upholstered in orange fabric, complete the retro-modern look.

To create the dining rotunda, Kester Inc and Architecture TM removed a large central support column, replacing it with several steel trusses dotted throughout the space. The star-studded 7.6 metre (25 foot) wide dome is formed from seven wedge-shaped, pre-cast gypsum panels suspended from the ceiling. The starry effect is created by coloured neon light, diffuse and changing, which is filtered through perforations fitted with clear resin to radiate a gentle glow.

Although this 'arena' provides plenty of scope for voyeurism, a degree of intimacy is created by the hand-cut, translucent resin screens inspired by Harry Bertoia's geometric *Multiplane* sculptures of the late 1950s and 1960s. Composed of linen sandwiched between gold and orange resin panels, from a distance it resembles a painted artwork, or a patchwork of parchment. Cocooning diners, the screens permit only tantalizing glimpses of the kitchen, bar and circulation routes beyond.

Additional dining space is provided by raised booths around the periphery of the rotunda and two small private dining rooms that open onto an outdoor patio. The basement houses the restrooms, a lounge and several private dining salons, but there's no doubt the only place to really experience Frisson dining is in the golden inner circle.

LEFT
The glamour of ocean liners of the 1920s and 1930s provided inspiration.

BELOW
Plan of the ground-floor level of the supper club, which occupies 836 square metres (9,000 square feet) spread over the ground floor and basement of an office block.

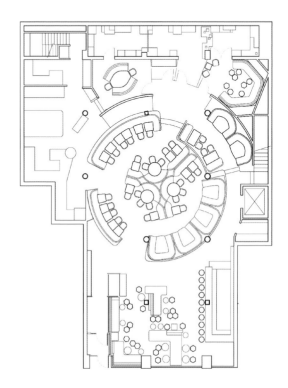

INN THE PARK

LONDON UK HOPKINS ARCHITECTS AND TOM DIXON

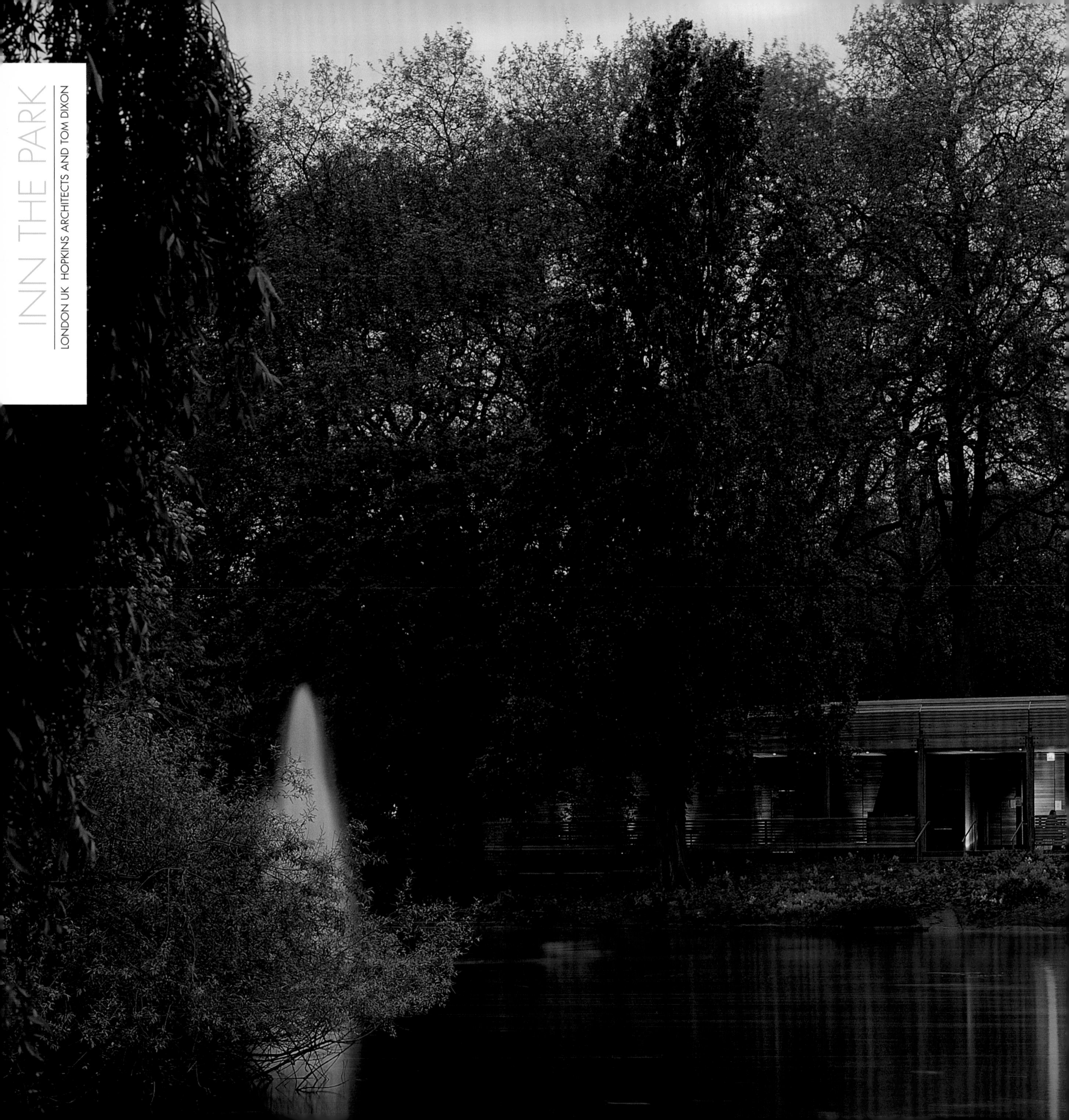

A masterpiece of British craftsmanship and design, the beauty of Inn the Park lies in its ability to blend in complete harmony with the landscape. Dubbed 'eco-chic', the timber construction is so artfully embedded within the gentle rolling landscape of John Nash's St James's Park that it appears to have emerged organically. It opened in April 2004 and was an initiative of the Royal Parks Agency, who commissioned the award-winning London-based Hopkins Architects in 1998 to create an equally democratic alternative to the existing, popular 1960s-built Cake House café. Their brief asked for a 'high-quality and elegant low-profile building, which nevertheless must advertise its presence'.

Hopkins Architects' subtle solution was achieved by studying the history of the park, which is one of London's oldest Royal Parks, dating back to 1828. The architects argued that Nash did not originally envisage pavilions in his park, and instead let the existing curves of the surrounding parkland dictate the architecture. 'The new building derives its form from the geometry of the landscape, in both plan and section,' writes Hopkins. 'At a point of convergence where two paths meet, the double curved plan creates a lozenge-shaped space set within a gently rising hillock.'

The £2 million (around $3.5 million) outcome is a low-slung concrete and timber construction clad in Austrian Larch with a sweeping layered frontage bordered by a lakeside path. Hopkins Architects layered the lakeside frontage with a long public bench followed by an elevated level comprising a sheltered outdoor 120-seat terrace. Finally, set behind glazed sliding doors is the 100-cover restaurant with the kitchen at the rear. The architects burrowed the storage underground and concealed the sloping rear of the structure beneath a grassy landscaped hillock. Approaching from The Mall, the structure is camouflaged by rolling grassy parkland, whereas from the front its low, timber colonnade appears as a minimal intervention – a simple unobtrusive shelter beneath the trees.

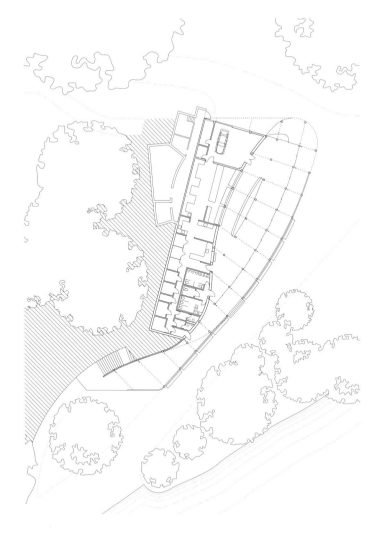

Very much the modern British café, Inn the Park, run by seasoned restaurateur Oliver Peyton's company Grupo, is part of the new wave of British restaurants celebrating national dishes made from regional, often organic, produce. It is fitting, then, that British designer Tom Dixon OBE should be responsible for the fit-out. Inside, he provided some aesthetic respite from the acres of wood by inserting a row of white marble booths furnished with black leather banquettes. These also provide internal order, aiding customer circulation by providing a partition between the busy, take-away 'grab and go' buffet area and the calmer dining area.

The furniture – all designed by Dixon – lends a distinctly mid-century modern feel: tubular stainless-steel chairs with black or purple mock-croc leather cushions and tables with burgundy stove enamel tops. Terrace furniture continues the theme, with wire-framed chairs and marble-topped tables. The abundance of glazing, and a series of skylights, reduces the need for complex lighting; in keeping with the modern chrome and steel furnishings but also the organic curves of the architecture, Dixon's own 'Mirror Ball' pendants set the interior warmly aglow at night.

LEFT
Handblown glass discs
attached to aluminium rods
screen off a 40-seat dining
area.

TOP, CENTRE AND
BOTTOM RIGHT
Copper Bleu's extraordinary
copper-clad façade is
visible from the nearby
highway and designed
specifically to attract
attention.

Burnished by the sun, Copper Bleu cuts a distinctive, undulating copper form in the Minnesota landscape. Located close to the intersection of two highways, in an area that was once prairie grasses and farmland but is now a growing, affluent suburb of Minneapolis, the 'Modern American Bistro' opened in December 2005. It took multidisciplinary Chicago-based firm Jordan Mozer Associates (JMA) – who have designed several restaurants, including Herzblut in Hamburg (featured in *Restaurant Design*, 2004) – 18 months to create the new-build.

Building was preceded by a period of indepth research into the surrounding area and potential demographic, during which JMA discovered that Minnesota citizens, although culturally diverse and well versed in contemporary global culinary trends, also enjoyed the simple life found in the great outdoors, many spending weekends at their lake houses, camping and fishing. To attract these local residents, Jordan Mozer says, 'the brief required a guest experience that was at once familiar and new, rooted in local Midwestern culture and mid-century restaurant archetypes, but modern, sophisticated and globally influenced.'

Working together with JMA architect Jeff Carloss, Mozer conceived Copper Bleu using regional materials and construction methods. 'We took stone, copper and wood and we created the rustic variation of an "upscale casual" restaurant. In some ways you could categorize it as Frank Lloyd Wright modern with a twist. We've taken Wright modernism and given another interpretation to what organic means; it's a bit more expressionist than strictly modern,' explains Mozer.

A powerful street presence was vital, since the site was sunken 4.3 metres (14 feet) below highway level. JMA conceived a 650 square metre (7,000 square foot) plan that is the fusion of two copper-clad, stone-based buildings with gently rolling roofs that snake around a landscaped garden of dense evergreens, providing a natural barrier between the restaurant and the highway. The restaurant entrance is marked by a twisting copper canopy that cuts through to become the ceiling of the reception area inside.

Copper Bleu's interior bears all the hallmarks of a Jordan Mozer creation. Virtually everything was custom-made specifically for the project. Curvaceous forms and unique sculptural elements – from the bulbous steel greeter's desk to the polished aluminium brackets supporting milk-acrylic shelves for the back bar bottle display – adding an idiosyncratic dimension. Comforting, familiar materials that patinate well, including Brazilian ebony, mesquite, mahogany

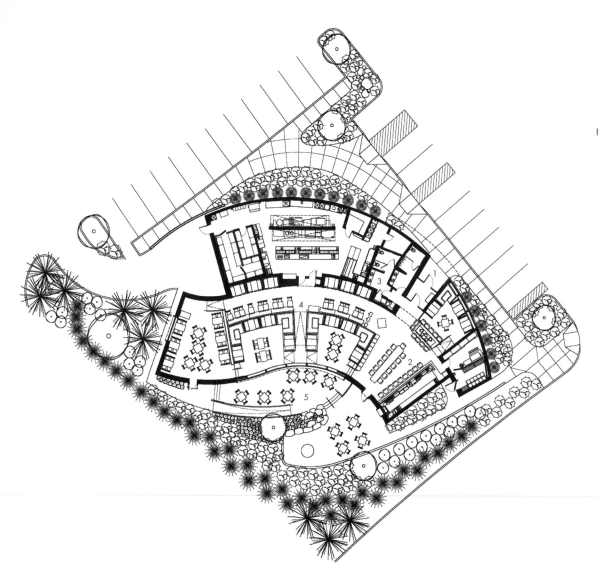

and bronze, were deliberately chosen throughout to create a warm, inviting atmosphere.

The restaurant seats 218 in total and is housed within a long, winding, fluid space that wraps around the garden and patio. To maintain an informal atmosphere, JMA integrated the bar and lounge, positioning them near the entrance. The ceiling emphasizes the flowing nature of the architecture: 'this is composed of Douglas Fir beams arranged undulating and radiating to support the curved roof, which is composed of hyberbolic parabola shapes,' explains Mozer. Bespoke lighting heightens the effect, with a dozen 6 metre (20 foot) long, steel-framed chandeliers supporting individually lit glass cylinders – 25,000 in total – inserted at regular intervals between the beams.

Seating is organized into two large bays of fixed banquettes. A more intimate 40-seat dining area at the far end is made semi-private by a screen of hand-blown glass discs, attached to polished aluminium columns and topped by specially cast spiral cap-nuts. Tables throughout are solid mahogany and chairs are upholstered in chocolate brown velvet. Although inspired by mid-century modern steak house chairs, these have gently winged backs that lend them a quirky, distinctively Mozeresque life of their own.

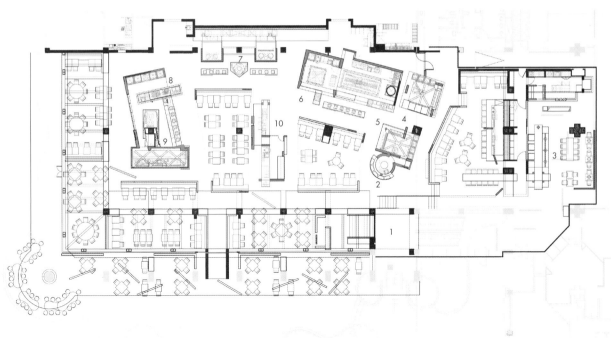

The Line, in Singapore's Shangri-La Hotel, is the brave new twenty-first-century version of the buffet restaurant typically found in five-star Asian hotels. It opened in March 2005 and was created by Adam D. Tihany, who has been designing high-profile restaurants for 25 years – many in his adopted home city of New York – for top chefs such as Wolfgang Puck, Jean-Georges Vongerichten and Thomas Keller. 'Singapore has a long tradition of absolutely spectacular food,' says Tihany, 'and in terms of market style buffets, the benchmark for a long time was Mezza9 in the Grand Hyatt by Super Potato. My directive from the Shangri-La group was to reinterpret the concept and to build the next big thing.'

In contrast to Mezza9, which is moody, dark and dramatic, with an abundance of signature Super Potato organic materials such as rock and glass, Tihany conjured up something entirely different. 'It's the iPod of buffets, very today and ultra contemporary, sleek and light. It's clean, open and joyous,' he says. The all-day self-service dining room is located in the Lower Lobby Level of the hotel and accommodates 390 diners. Predominantly white, with pearlescent silver vinyl and white leather banquettes and chairs, The Line has an almost space-age appeal. Glowing orange vertical and horizontal light boxes inserted throughout create a cohesive identity in a 1,115 square metre (12,000 square foot) space that houses a dozen pavilions with display kitchens serving a variety of food types from Italian to sushi. The pavilions are constructed from high-tech

materials – white Corian counters are finished with mirror polished stainless-steel and glass to showcase the food.

'The concept behind The Line is not a line of people standing,' explains Tihany, 'it's a lifeline, the connection between all of us and nature and food, the whole story.' Four short art films were commissioned from Tihany's son Bram, a movie director, in keeping with this theme. *Vegetables*, *Fish*, *Grain* and *Wine*, which are projected on 2.7 metre (9-foot) long plasma screens that form a backdrop to the food stations, explore and celebrate the relationship between natural produce and food. 'The movies really show you how to make bread and wine, they're really inspirational,' explains Tihany senior. 'Environmental issues are not going away, they are going to get worse and the connection is topical. There's a sort of a message there that if we're not good to nature then nature won't be good to us and we won't be able to enjoy the bounties.'

LEFT
Silver vinyl seating reinforces the contemporary, clean look.

ABOVE
Plan. 1. entrance, 2. crustacean counter, 3. coffee/cake, 4. Thai salad, 5. sushi/sashimi, 6. western, 7. dim sum/wok/ steamer, 8. satay/tandoori, 9. soup noodle, 10. dessert.

Ever since Frank Gehry's silver Guggenheim boosted the fortunes of Bilbao it has prompted commissions for astounding new public architecture in cities around the world. Even existing institutions are undergoing renovation, or receiving impressive extensions by headline architects. A major part of this bid by museums to attract and retain visitors includes updating any additional revenue-generating offerings too, in particular the restaurants. Even a popular, well-established museum such as the Museum of Modern Art (MoMA) in midtown Manhattan recently underwent serious renovation, which includes a new wing by Japanese architect Yoshio Taniguchi and a new restaurant, aptly titled The Modern.

Keen to create the best restaurant possible, one that would attract both museum patrons and the general public, MoMA employed reputable restaurateurs, the Union Square Hospitality Group, to run the operation, and commissioned top architects Bentel & Bentel to design the 930 square metre (10,000 square foot) space. Bentel & Bentel have designed several high-profile restaurants including Craft, also in New York. The Modern, which opened in November 2004, is located at the nexus between the original 1937 building by Stone and Goodwin, the adjacent 1964 annex and Sculpture Garden by Philip Johnson, and the new Taniguchi wing.

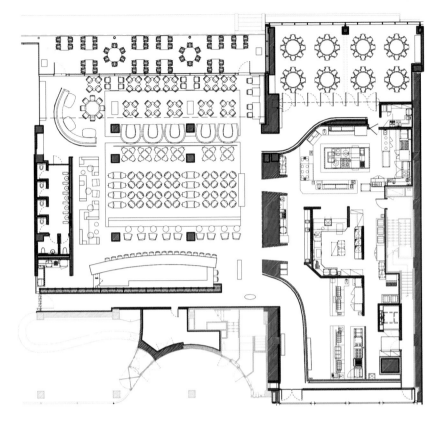

Although accessible from the museum, a separate, discreet street entrance nearby secures The Modern's independent status. Guests enter via a curved corridor, defined by a simple, white luminous glass wall – a hint of things to come. As its name suggests, the interior is a serenely clean space, free of extraneous clutter. Lighting elements are either concealed within ceiling slots or incorporated within structural elements.

Peter Bentel explains: 'There are no decorative light fixtures – instead, we use light as one of the elements of our material palette. For instance, the system of luminous walls that weave the spaces of the restaurant together provide light within the restaurant while creating a weightless contrast to the materiality of the hand-polished stainless steel, black terrazzo, bronze glass and rift-sawn white oak used throughout.' All restaurant services, such as air-conditioning, speakers and sprinklers, are secreted behind glossy, white stretched-PVC ceiling panels, thus allowing the interior's clean lines to flourish.

Bentel & Bentel have organized the 322-capacity restaurant into two areas; the Barroom which includes informal dining and The Modern, a fine-dining restaurant (with an outdoor terrace), which overlooks the Sculpture Garden. The reduced colour scheme reinforces an appreciation of the materials, finishes and furnishings that serve to define the two spaces. It also intensifies (especially with red as the only accent colour) and throws into almost hyper-real relief the verdant photographic mural of trees by the artist Thomas Demand. The mural fills one end of the Barroom, imbuing it with a mirage quality, like a genuine view into a forest.

The 'luminous walls', such as the etched-glass screen separating the fine- and informal dining rooms, also bind the individual spaces together. For example, the gently curving bar of backlit frosted glass topped by white arabescato marble visually bookends the etched-glass screen, thus containing the Barroom within ephemeral, light-giving boundaries. Bentel says: 'these gauze-like veils of luminous glass reiterate, along with other significant design elements such as the all-glass wine display, the brushed-marble bar and the custom-designed seating, the desire to create a spare yet warm series of interior dining environments.' Surfaces maximize light; the polished black terrazzo floor extends the radiance of the bar and support columns are rendered virtually invisible by virtue of their mirrored cladding that generates distorted reflections.

The architects have used fixed furniture to define areas: 'we used large pieces as architectural elements', says Bentel. The bar is clearly distinguished from the informal dining area by a low, black leather banquette on the bar side, combined with an inset of light oak flooring in the dining section. Bespoke, freestanding cabinetry of white oak and marble, which functions as waiters' stations, serve a similar purpose.

The Modern dining room benefits from double-height ceilings and glazing affording a prime view of the Sculpture Garden. An executive blue carpet and the standard white linen adds to the formal dining feel. Power-dining booths of black-brown leather were custom-designed by Bentel & Bentel to match the Arne Jacobsen 'Oxford' dining chairs.

It is the array of Danish furniture classics that reinforces the thoroughly modern, mid-century aesthetic. 'The Danish government bestowed on the museum a generous gift that stipulated the use of Danish design,' explains Bentel. 'After two scouting trips to Denmark, we selected a number of older Danish modern classics – such as Jacobsen's "Oxford" chair in brown leather and polished aluminium [in The Modern] and Poul Kjaerholm's "PK-9" chair in brushed stainless steel and black leather [in the Barroom] – and combined them with contemporary designs such as Flemming Busk's "Lotus" lounge chair in red leather and stainless steel.'

FAR LEFT
Alfresco diners can admire MoMA's sculpture garden at the rear.

LEFT
The plan shows a restaurant of two halves; the informal Barroom (bottom left of plan) precedes the more serious fine-dining room (top).

RIGHT
Arne Jacobsen's 'Oxford' dining chairs are paired with bespoke booths by Bentel & Bentel in the fine-dining room.

Barcelona's restaurant scene has undergone a serious renaissance of late, receiving international press attention for its avant-garde tapas, spearheaded somewhat by the fame of El Bulli – the restaurant just north of the city where devoted foodies make pilgrimages to sample the weird and wonderful experimental creations of globally revered chef Ferran Adrià. Back in the city, there are many contemporary chef-run establishments that are being lauded for their cuisine, such as Comerç 24 (featured in *Restaurant Design*), which is run by Adrià protégé chef Carles Abellan. There is also Grupo Tragaluz, a family-run company that operates more than a dozen hip, designer contemporary restaurants, such as El Japonès, Agua and Bestial, often with equally progressive cuisine.

Moo is located in the group' s first hotel venture, the boutique Hotel Omm, which opened in December 2003. Centrally located, the hotel is just off the famous Paseig de Grácia in the exclusive Eixample district, not far from Gaudí' s residential masterpiece, La Pedrera. Grupo Tragaluz' s restaurant and bar interiors are designed by in-house duo, Sandra Tarruella and Isabel López. Moo is located at the rear of the open-plan lobby, behind the hotel's striking silver façade of Cabra marble, designed by Catalan architect Juli Capella and featuring windows and balconies that teasingly curl open like the doors of an advent calendar.

Moo is overseen by the Roca brothers, of Girona's critically acclaimed Cellar Can Roca. Their cuisine is very much in the experimental avant-garde tapas vein; diners are encouraged to try five courses each paired with a different wine. Desserts include dishes designed to emulate the taste of designer perfumes – such as Calvin Klein's Eternity – delivered with a sample of the scent to compare flavour.

Tarruella and López's interior is fittingly contemporary, with much of the hotel displaying a Scandinavian-influenced design of clean lines and light blonde timber. The open-plan lobby benefits from natural light filtered through nine pyramidal skylights. Moo is discreetly separated from the front lounge and central bar by a central floating metallic mesh screen, allowing views between areas. Roughly textured plaster walls are uplit and lined with timber slats that diffuse the light to generate a gentle warm glow. Blonde bentwood 'Kayak' dining chairs designed by Jorgi Pensi are very much in keeping with the Scandinavian aesthetic.

Little colour or decoration is necessary since Moo's focal point is its verdant backdrop, clearly visible through floor-to-ceiling glazing. This narrow exterior courtyard encased behind glass houses an abstract landscape design by Beth Figueras, composed of sedum, Buddhist prayer poles that resemble bamboo and giant mirrors reminiscent of water lilies, which deflect natural light into Moo. Viewed from a distance the composition, set against a white wall, resembles a two-dimensional, oversized piece of wallpaper. The courtyard is a refreshing solution, creating a restaurant that feels light filled and with some aspect in an otherwise compact, low-ceilinged space. Both the food and design are evidently working well – within a year of opening Moo won its first Michelin star.

LEFT
Natural light floods in from the outdoor courtyard through floor-to-ceiling glazing.

ABOVE
Beth Figueras's landscaping is part garden and part artwork. Organically shaped mirrors reflect light into the restaurant.

CANTEEN
LONDON UK UNIVERSAL DESIGN STUDIO

CAN

Opening times
Monday to Friday
11am–11pm
Saturday to Sunday
9am–11pm
0845 686 1122
www.canteen.co.uk

Restaurants with a jaw-dropping 'wow factor' are always a thrill, but sometimes the best designed places are those where the surroundings are so user-friendly that they enhance the dining experience without making a song and dance about it. Canteen, in the new Foster + Partners Spitalfields market development in east London, is one such place; it oozes the essence of 'good design' that was so enthusiastically pioneered during the post-war years. Canteen opened in October 2005 and is part of a new wave of restaurants championing British regional produce and cooking that have opened in the UK in recent years.

The trio behind Canteen – Patrick Clayton-Malone, Cass Titcombe and Dominic Lake – considered their 'democratic eating house' concept, which would celebrate the best of British food and craftsmanship, for 18 months before they appointed Universal Design Studio to execute their comprehensive 80-page brief. 'We were very prescriptive', says Clayton-Malone. 'Ultimately we wanted an emphasis on simple, high quality materials that reference the optimism of mid-century design and the classlessness of community spaces like the Royal Festival Hall, town halls and libraries. Longevity was important, we wanted it to last and not date'.

Universal Design Studio, perhaps better known for their retail projects for Stella McCartney and Juicy Couture, were chosen for their 'sensibility of simplicity'. The multi-disciplinary practice is headed by architect Jonathan Clarke, together with Edward Barber and Jay Osgerby, the successful furniture-design duo. Universal achieved the

honest, 'minimum of frills' look that the clients desired through an economic palette of classic, durable materials – oak, linoleum, ceramic, cork floor tiles and Portoro Italian marble inside and out – which all lend a somewhat nostalgic sense of longevity. Furniture is beautifully basic; simple oak communal refectory-style tables (larger scale versions of BarberOsgerby's 'Home' table) are paired with the designers' 'Portsmouth' benches. The more intimate window seats are made cosier by banquettes upholstered in an olive green fabric by Bute.

Canteen manages to feel utilitarian without being overtly industrial, and democratic without being cheap. Jonathan Clarke of Universal explains, 'We wanted democratic efficiency, but we didn't want to create a fast-food restaurant with high seating or brash lighting; it needed to reflect the quality of the food. We've made it far more luxurious and comfortable through subtle things, such as lower seating levels, the depth of seating and the thickness of the tables.'

The past proved a rich source of inspiration when looking to satisfy the owners' request that the restaurant be informal, efficient and user-led. 'We studied the materials and design of railway carriages, when train travel was a glamorous experience and thought about how there were always places to put your things,' says Clarke. The results are in the details such as the handy coatrails slotted between each window seating 'compartment', the sliding Corian trays (for keys, mobile phones and the like) and the ceramic 'Hector' lamps that add a warm glow to the window-side tables.

The space – essentially a glass box glazed on three sides – presented a challenge for lighting. 'It was tricky because there's an abundance of natural light,' says Clarke, 'so we dropped the lighting levels, creating warmth and intimacy. Some people have compared it to a Hopperesque diner feel.' All lighting elements were custom-made and deliberately understated. Three metre (9 feet 8 inch) wide horizontal linear pendants in a folded aluminium design are suspended to hang low above the large communal tables. 'The design is about subtlety and simplicity, and by focusing the lighting on the food and diner's faces and hands this character is given to the restaurant,' says Simpson. Such considered lighting also manages to create a sense of intimacy even when diners might be eating communally among strangers.

PREVIOUS PAGE

Echoes of *Nighthawks*: an external view of Canteen in the new Spitalfields market development.

THIS PAGE

LEFT
Ceramic 'Hector' lamps help create a sense of intimacy and warmth despite the floor-to-ceiling glazing.

RIGHT
Nostalgia for early train travel led the designers to create 'places to put your things' such as sliding trays and coat rails.

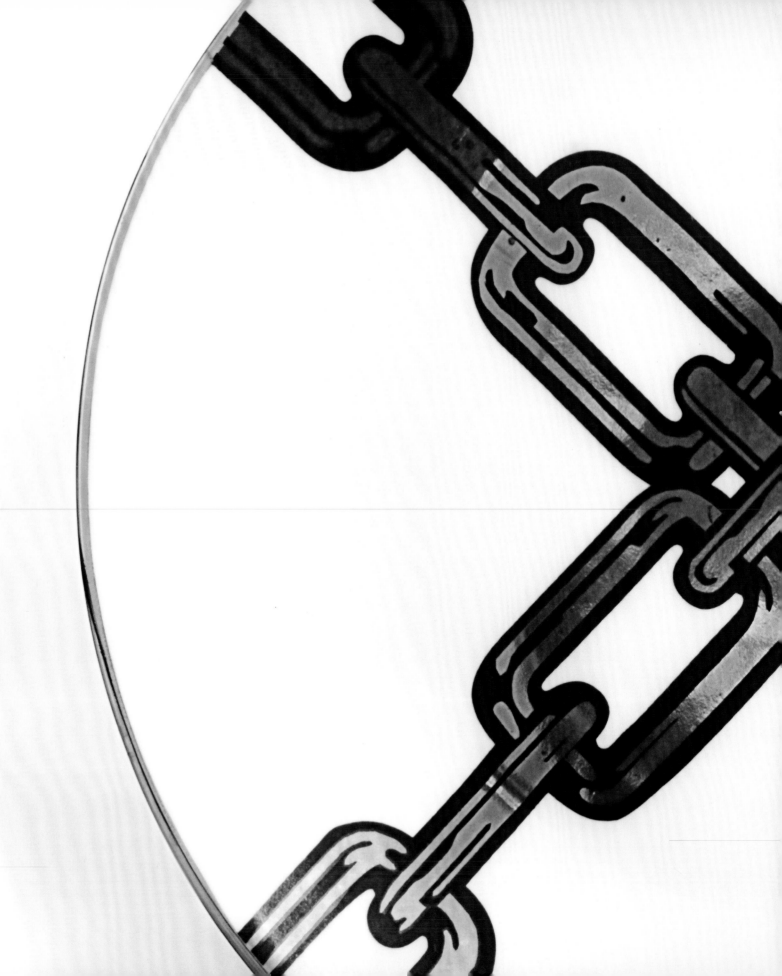

LEFT
The sleek, modern furnishings contrast strikingly with the original Louis Majorelle wood panelling.

RIGHT
Lounge alcoves are decorated with an Asian-modern theme.

Whereas many chefs might strive for Michelin star status, other Michelin-starred veterans are only too keen to fling them aside. There was Joël Robuchon's retirement from his three-star Paris restaurant in 1996 and subsequent seven-year hiatus from the stoves, and then in May 2005 fellow Frenchman Alain Senderens, a Michelin-starred chef for 28 years, announced that he too was relinquishing his stars by closing his 'pompous restaurant' Lucas Carton on the place de la Madeleine in the 8th arrondissement. At the time Senderens was quoted as saying: 'I don't want to compete any more, I am 65 years old, and I want to have some fun.' Instead, he decided to transform Lucas Carton into a contemporary, informal restaurant offering 'three-star quality' food at a quarter of the price of the original.

Such a transformation required a new look. Young French designer Noé Duchaufour Lawrance, who was responsible for the ground-floor spaces at London's Sketch, was commissioned to contemporize the existing Art Nouveau interior, originally created in 1910 by decorator and furniture designer Louis Majorelle. Senderens's brief requested that the new restaurant evoke rebirth, or more specifically, the 'emergence from a chrysalis'. Duchaufour Lawrance's new design was unveiled in September 2005 and the new 80-seat dining room reveals a sensual blending of ultra modern, almost futuristic, furniture and lighting details with the flowing natural forms of Majorelle's lemon and sycamore wood panelling.

Glowing Barrisol ceiling panels, designed to resemble silk chrysali, emit a gently diffused light in each dining alcove. Decorative details by Korean artist Yoon Hee Ahn reflecting the Asian influence in Senderens's new menu – luminous Art Nouveau-style butterflies and irises adorn Perspex panels, which are layered against the mirrored walls and the tops of the white composite marble tables. Chairs designed especially by Duchaufour Lawrance display an abstract wing-shaped back, in keeping with the butterfly theme.

The first floor comprises Le Passage Bar, which accommodates 40 patrons, as well as two small, 12-person lounges (the Salons Gris) and a salon privé (La Madeleine Lounge) seating eight. These spaces are entirely new, with only contemporary references to the restaurant's history. Le Passage Bar is wrapped in a curvaceous shell lined in bamboo panelling, while seating alcoves are finished in copper leaf that radiates a burnished glow.

In addition to the general lighting that is recessed behind the edges of the bamboo shell,

Duchaufour Lawrance has designed his own twenty-first-century chandeliers in collaboration with Baccarat: a series of illuminated Perspex panels suspended from the ceiling display engravings of nineteenth-century carafes, chandeliers and other ornate objects sourced from Baccarat's archives. Meanwhile, La Madeleine Lounge is shrouded in diaphanous drapes that reveal ornate but empty ghostly frames, painted in grey onto the pink walls. Maarten Baas's burnt black chandelier adds a touch of mid-noughties baroque with its edgy, twisted gothic aesthetic.

Senderens may have emerged from its cocoon as a more affordable, more relaxed and hipper restaurant than Lucas Carton, but it seems some chefs just can't escape their destiny. In spite of Monsieur Senderens's protestations, within a year of opening the little red guide had already awarded the new restaurant two stars; so far he hasn't returned them yet.

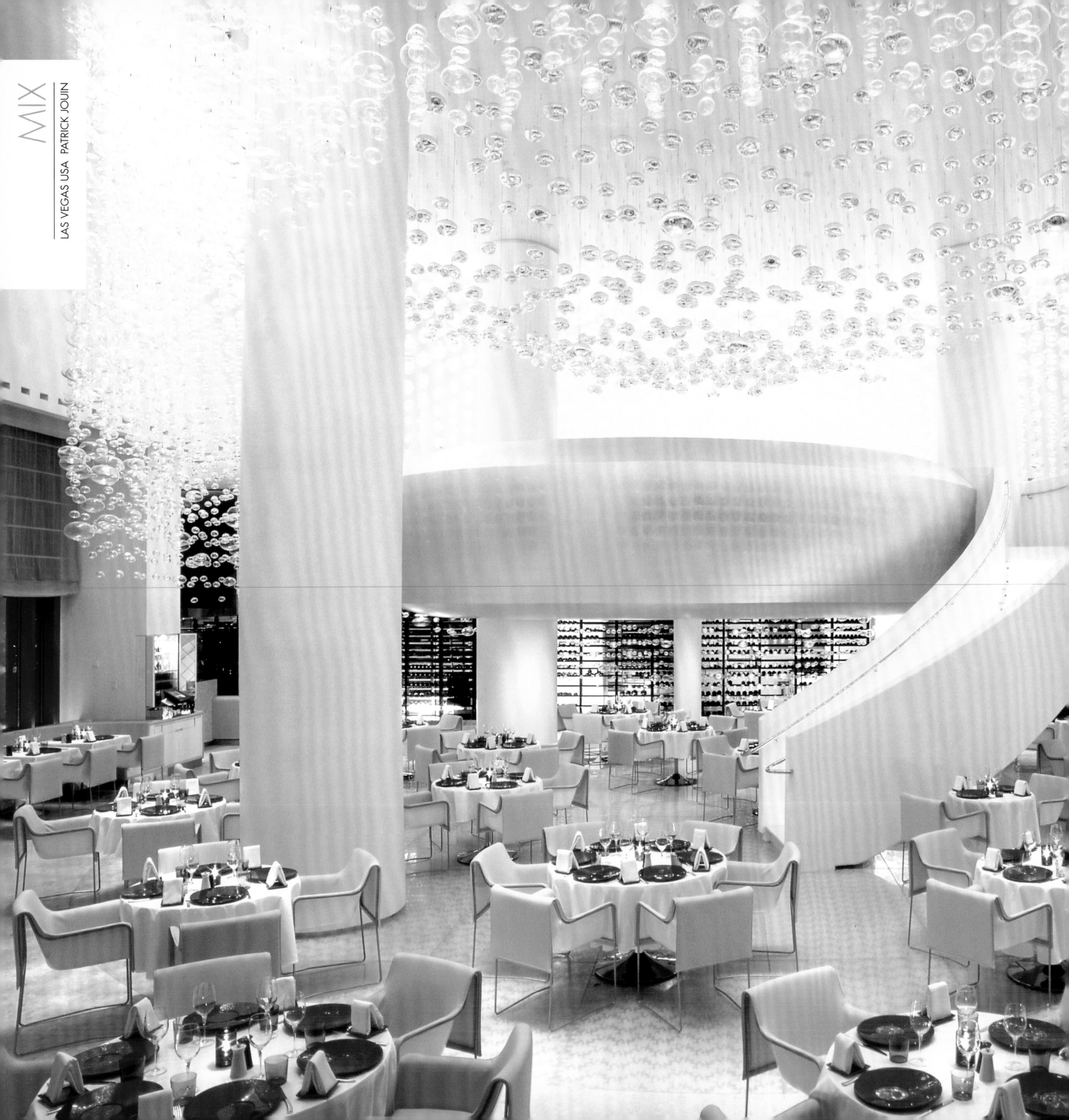

The collaboration between interior architect Patrick Jouin and international chef Alain Ducasse has resulted in the creation of many distinctive restaurants, from Plaza Athénée in Paris (2000) to Gilt in New York (2005; see pages 62–5), but perhaps most spectacular of all is the $15 million Mix in Las Vegas, which was completed in December 2004. This dramatic masterpiece is an ethereal vision of shimmering silver and white located at the top of THEhotel, the all-suite tower at the Mandalay Bay Resort & Casino. 'We had 12 metres (39 feet) of ceiling height and a fantastic view of Las Vegas, so our design had to compete with the view,' says Jouin, comparing the finished environment to 'like being in the clouds'.

The vast L-shaped space comprises a 200-seat restaurant with a 40-seat outdoor terrace and a 300-capacity lounge bar, also with a 40-seat terrace; an open kitchen situated between the two was 'deliberately designed to preserve their distinctive identities'. Diners arrive via an elevator and pass through a dark, rust-coloured corridor before stepping into the dazzling light of the futuristic two-storey dining room. At its heart is a circular dining mezzanine clad in silver-leaf and encircled by a shower of 15,000 hand-blown Murano glass bubbles cascading from the ceiling. Beneath these transparent floating bubbles tables, dressed in white linen, are paired with bespoke 'Mabelle' chairs, upholstered in ultra-modern white faux leather. Around the perimeter of the room are several dining pods, or high-backed booths, their concave interiors lined in gleaming silver leaf, giving them the air of sci-fi satellites 'circling' the central mezzanine.

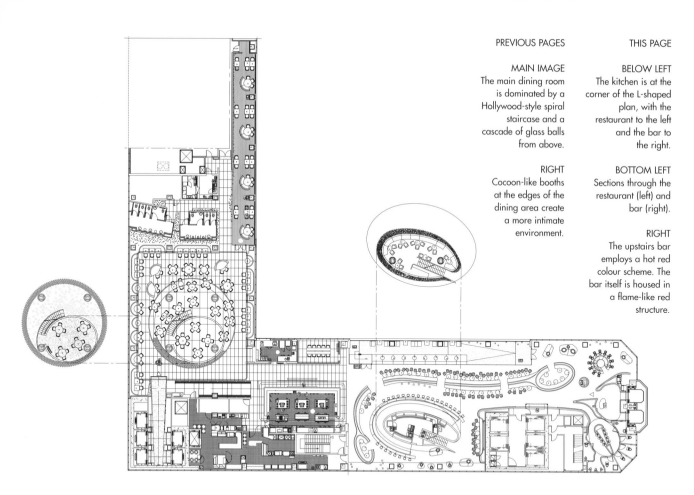

PREVIOUS PAGES

MAIN IMAGE
The main dining room is dominated by a Hollywood-style spiral staircase and a cascade of glass balls from above.

RIGHT
Cocoon-like booths at the edges of the dining area create a more intimate environment.

THIS PAGE

BELOW LEFT
The kitchen is at the corner of the L-shaped plan, with the restaurant to the left and the bar to the right.

BOTTOM LEFT
Sections through the restaurant (left) and bar (right).

RIGHT
The upstairs bar employs a hot red colour scheme. The bar itself is housed in a flame-like red structure.

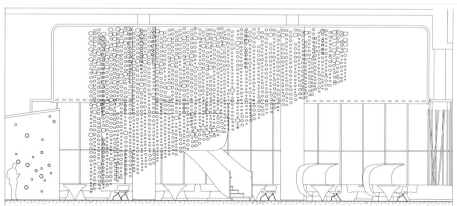

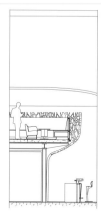

By contrast, the lounge bar is a study in fiery scarlet, the moodier hell to the silvery celestial heaven of the dining space. Jouin's studio describe the distinction rather poetically: 'The deep, sexy, entrancing red in the bowels of the bar, and the purity of whiteness, translucent, in suspension as airy as the skies, in the restaurant.' Echoing the restaurant, the lounge is dominated by a two-storey centrepiece, an oval bar, the central core of which rises up into an organic tree-like construction that's been likened to 'a bouquet of coral' and 'a vision of magma'. The red-lacquered structure is composed of fibreglass supported by a metal frame and was installed by helicopter through a hole in the roof of the tower. A stairway to the rear of the bar provides access to the bar's mezzanine enclosure, where VIPs can spy down on fellow drinkers and take in glittering views of Las Vegas through the branch-like fibres of Jouin's unique parapet.

LEFT
Views through
to the restaurant
from the club
space.

ABOVE
Large green
panels flip down
to separate the
club from the
restaurant.

Not every restaurant is designed to last. In fact, a very recent trend, following in the footsteps of the retail industry, has been the guerrilla restaurant: temporary dining spaces designed to make a fleeting appearance for a season. Many, such as Mist in Antwerp and Together in Amsterdam, are open only for one summer, while London's The Reindeer, designed by a bevy of fashionistas, existed for just one month before Christmas 2006. In many of these examples, it seems, a shorter shelf-life can guarantee a level of exclusivity and hipness that longevity cannot.

Restaurant Bar Club 11 in Amsterdam was built to last only two years, a good deal longer than the new flash-in-the-pan breed of guerrilla restaurant. The multi-purpose restaurant/club/art/exhibition space has, however, proved a great success since opening in May 2004 and the lease has been extended until July 2008. It is located on Oosterdokskade, a brief walk from Amsterdam's central station, and occupies the eleventh floor of the former post office headquarters. Identifiable by huge lettering reading POST CS, this industrial office block is also a temporary home to the Stedelijk Museum, which specializes in modern art and design, as well as to several art and design companies, lending the location an edgy, creative feel.

Restaurant Bar Club 11 was inventively designed with a minimal budget of 250,000 Euros. 'Our ambition was to create a large space with big-city allure that would be unique in Amsterdam. Created with monumental gestures and a low-budget approach, it has become a special and yet accessible space with an aura of freedom,' says Bas Van Tol. Nature – or at least the great outdoors – provided much inspiration, resulting in a verdant and earthy colour scheme and some innovative Droog-like recycling, such as tree-trunk stumps for furniture in the club, picnic benches in the restaurant and lighting features composed of terracotta-coloured plastic plant pots and saucers.

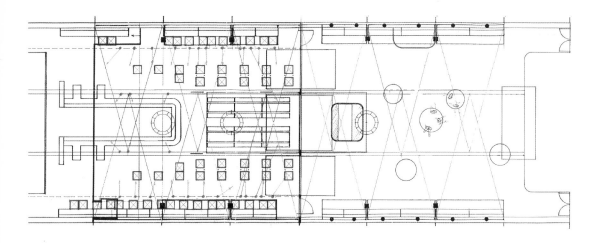

ABOVE
Plan of the 750
square metre (8,072
square foot) space,
which has been
divided equally
between the club
and the dining area.

LEFT
Projections play on
banks of screens
lining the walls
above the windows.

RIGHT
A view of 11 at
night from the
dining mezzanine.

Playing to their advantage of sky-high views (few restaurants in low-rise Amsterdam boast such vistas), the designers maintained an open-plan feel and broad industrial-scale windows. The only divisions, aside from that enclosing the open kitchen, are the flexible 'up-and-over' green felt panels that can be used to separate the restaurant from the club. When open, these form a horizontal division that is level with the rear dining mezzanine, and they also echo the split between the two panoramas offered to guests: the natural view from the window and the visuals on the rows of large video screens above.

At the centre of the restaurant is a lemon yellow island bar and an elevated seating platform which maximizes window views for diners seated on the picnic benches. Long banquettes line the windows, and additional seating is provided by Patricia Urquiola's 'Fjord' bucket chairs in ivory. Bringing the messy, industrial ceiling back down to earth in a rather spectacular fashion are two huge terracotta chandeliers. Quite a hotspot, with popular club nights from Thursday through Saturday, Restaurant Club Bar 11 is proof that spending millions and lasting forever is not the only recipe for success.

EVO

BARCELONA SPAIN RICHARD ROGERS PARTNERSHIP, ALONSO I BALAGUER ARQUITECTES AND GCA ARQUITECTES ASSOCIATS

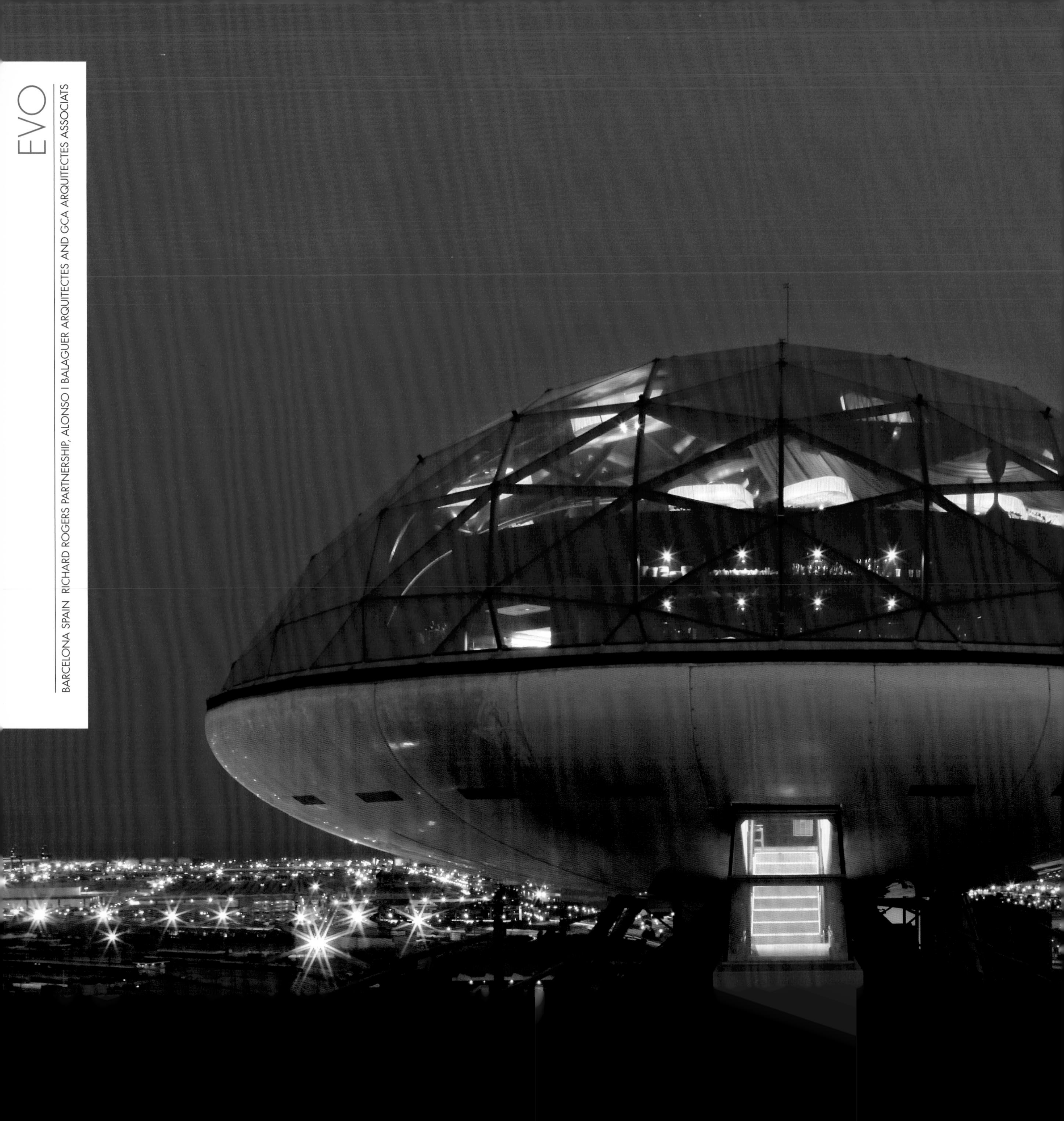

Evo appears to hover above the Hesperia Hotel tower like a passing UFO. The glass geodesic dome is the cherry on top of the 75 million Euro (£50.3 million), 105-metre (344 foot) high hotel designed by Richard Rogers Partnership in collaboration with Spanish architects Alonso i Balaguer. Taller than anything for miles around, the Hesperia is six minutes from the airport, and borders the busy Avenida de la Granvía motorway in L'Hospitalet de Llobregat, a residential district on the outskirts of Barcelona that is undergoing considerable gentrification. In typical Rogers style, the brutal red-accented concrete hotel wears its services on its sleeve; the fire-escape stairs on one side glint like futuristic vertebrae while Evo sits on top, resembling a satellite pod ready for lift off at any moment.

Accessible via its own dedicated mini-elevator from an upper floor, the space-age eyrie houses the exclusive 75-cover restaurant of three-star Michelin chef Santi Santamaria of Can Fabes fame. The interior, like the rest of the hotel, was designed by GCA Arquitectes Associats, a firm with more than 20 years' experience in contemporary hotel design. Within the 267 square metre (2,874 square foot) circular space GCA has created three different levels 'to solve circulation problems, while giving privacy and identity to the tables' location.' Guests enter the first level, a 'perimetral passage' from which the upper levels are

LEFT
Close encounters of the Evo kind atop the Hesperia tower.

ABOVE
A separate elevator at the top whisks diners up to the restaurant.

LEFT AND RIGHT
Lights arch up like sci-fi sunflowers.

BELOW
The plan shows how most tables line the perimeter. At the centre is the show kitchen surrounded by a bar for diners.

BOTTOM
Section through the restaurant. Several concentric levels have been created within the dome.

accessible via stairs, or a ramp. The majority of dining tables run around the C-shaped second level. Above this is the third level, housing a central show kitchen – where diners can sit on stools to witness the culinary skills of the chefs – as well as an 18-seat private dining area.

Decoration in such a vista-abundant space would be superfluous, and GCA has wisely kept furniture simple and the palette neutral. In keeping with the remainder of the hotel, tables are lacquered a glossy black, and cream chairs by Artifort echo the circular host dome. Lighting was a challenge. Determined not to obstruct the panoramic views, GCA designed stainless-steel-framed lamps – reminiscent of Castiglioni's classic 'Arco' – which, from the perimeter, arch into the space to project light onto each table. Their golden yellow, rhomboid-shaped fabric shades also conceal within water sprinklers and speakers. Sprouting up over diners like alien sunflowers or surveillance androids, they reinforce the space-age aesthetic of the dome. Guests pay around 130 Euros for the privilege of gourmet dining on high, but with distances of up to 18 kilometres (11 miles) visible on a clear day, it is a roof top view that is hard to beat.

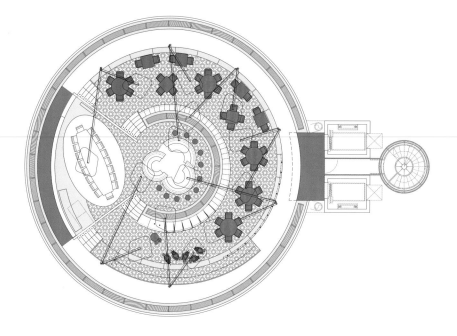

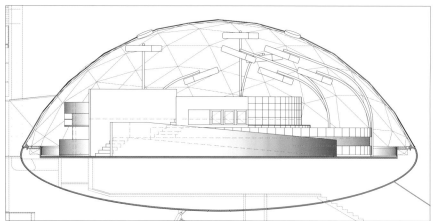

LEFT
Vidal's café, bar
and restaurant
below the glossy
underbelly of
Nouvel's
auditorium.

RIGHT
Low communal
furniture creates
a café-style
environment at
the front of the
space.

As the 'Bilbao Effect' continues, with famous architects creating iconic cultural institutions in major cities across the world, existing galleries and museums are gaining impressive new additions in a bid to attract visitors and maintain their landmark status. As these transformations occur, the remodelled interiors and extensions invariably include revenue-generating elements such as shops, cafés and restaurants. It is no longer sufficient to offer a basic canteen tucked away in the basement; the cosmopolitan public's appetite for decent food served in an attractive environment is resulting in some impressive new dining spaces.

Arola-Madrid – at the base of the 91 million, Jean Nouvel-designed wing of the Museo Reina Sofía – is a prime example of such a café-restaurant. Nouvel's extension to the existing gallery – a rather austere eighteenth-century building originally designed to be a hospital by Francesco Sabatini – is a triumvirate of glass and steel structures housing exhibition halls, a library and a 400-capacity auditorium, which are arranged to form a vast, irregularly shaped

courtyard. Nouvel has covered this transitory space with a glossy red canopy of zinc and red-lacquered aluminium, which he calls a 'unifying wing'. This is punctuated by rectangular slanted apertures that allow light to flood into the plaza and frame the sky, so that on glancing up, the canopy resembles a Matisse painting, or a hyper-real photograph.

The auditorium is the extension's most striking element – clearly visible through a glazed façade, it looms up bulbously like the futuristic monumental hull of a hovering space-ship. 'The auditorium and meeting rooms are unique because of their form, inherited from theatre typologies: 'a taut-skinned jewel box with curved angles, surrounded by foyer terraces,' says Nouvel. Slotted beneath this lustrous belly is the eponymous café-restaurant of Ferrán Adrià protégé and Michelin two-star chef Sergi Arola.

Rather than disappearing beneath the shadow of Nouvel's beast, the 890 square metre (9,580 square foot) café, bar and restaurant feels like a remarkably democratic and accessible space

that is as much urban lobby as dining room. Luis Vidal of Madrid-based Vidal y Asociados Arquitectos was responsible for the interior design and has introduced a human scale to the space, which has varying ceiling heights, as dictated by the sloping nature of the auditorium above.

Nouvel's symmetrical footprint includes two wing-like structural supports that arch up to meet the lowest section of the auditorium belly (effectively forming a more intimate area to the rear), alongside which Vidal has inserted two projecting, stainless-steel bars. Vidal's rhythmic response comprises communal café-style furniture at the loftier front of the space, raised furniture levels to complement the twin bars and moderate ceiling heights towards the middle, and lower seating levels to provide fine-dining in the intimate enclosure at the rear.

Vidal's sculptural, white Corian furniture and silver-and-chrome chairs enhance the existing urban industrial aesthetic of the reflective red surface above and the granite paved flooring throughout (extended from the courtyard and original Sabatini building). 'The café furniture has been designed as white stripes running across the space, varying in height to accommodate the different uses: support, seats, tables, bar,' Vidal explains. To the centre, a large configuration of white Corian slopes up to become the internally illuminated backbone of the fine-dining area, providing a glowing vertical support for diners seated on the banquettes.

In stark contrast to the organic red form above, the internal landscape is composed of a series of white, catwalk-like horizontal installations that are brilliantly utilitarian in their varying heights: adults use them as coffee tables and bar tops, teenagers recline against sloping sections as if they're sun-loungers and toddlers treat the surfaces as if they were playground equipment. By night the space operates as a sophisticated destination restaurant. Vidal y Asociados appear to have created the perfect dining model – flexibile and egalitarian – for this popular cultural institution.

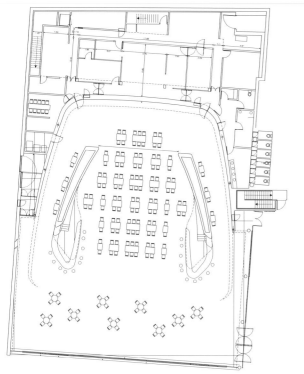

ABOVE LEFT
White Corian catwalks of varying heights provide communal tables and seating.

LEFT
The plan demonstrates that symmetry is all. The two bars flank the main dining area.

RIGHT
The fine-dining area is furnished with modular white tables and Viccarbe RS chairs of matt, chrome-finished steel and neoprene silver-finished fabric.

There can be few glittering city panoramas to rival that which greets diners at the Mediterranean restaurant Sirocco on the 63rd floor of the State Tower in Bangkok. This grand alfresco space, with its illuminated circular Sky Bar, sits high above the urban sprawl, giving guests spectacular far-reaching views of the capital. Sirocco is the only open-air element of this multi-faceted project that also comprises an Italian restaurant called Mezzaluna, the Distil Bar and the State Room function space. These are all housed within the dome construction that crowns the State Tower. The entire project was designed with a budget of 50,000,000 baht by the Bangkok office of dwp, a multidisciplinary firm with offices throughout the Far East.

Prior to the project's June 2004 completion, the 65-storey State Tower lay unoccupied for a decade, left undeveloped because of the Asian financial crisis. Today the Silom Road district is thriving again – in just 50 years this area has metamorphosed from paddy fields into the business and financial centre of Bangkok. Dense with financial institutions, offices of international companies, five-star hotels and designer boutiques, it is also home to Patpong, one of Bangkok's oldest nightlife districts for foreign visitors. And so it is the ideal spot for a landmark restaurant that offers newcomers such an impressive way to orientate themselves in an unfamiliar city.

Major structural alterations were required to complete the scheme. dwp raised the external floor by two metres (6 feet), which enabled them to construct the sweeping staircase that leads down from the elevators to the dining area, thus enhancing first impressions of the restaurant and adding that all-important opportunity for guests 'making an entrance'. Roman architecture was the inspiration, say dwp: 'the steps to the restaurant are a play on the Spanish Steps in Rome, complete with fountain.'

Adding drama are four internally uplit pillars. Inspired by the fluted columns of antiquity, these were originally designed to spray cool water as a form of air-conditioning but this has never been necessary. Constructed from steel poles, light is diffused through the pillars via hundreds of 2 centimetre (¾ inch) wide acrylic strips tethered at the top and bottom by stainless-steel wires.

An illuminated central table, similar to classic banqueting tables, reinforces the sense of symmetry. The timber and iron dining chairs are not particularly noteworthy but are durable, their oversized nature adding to the sense of grandeur. Glass balustrading ensures that nothing detracts from the vista.

At the end of the decked area, a raised platform, supported by a steel structure elevated 1.5 metres (5 feet) above the base concrete deck, houses the glowing star feature – the appropriately named Sky Bar. This circular laminated glass construction appears to float in the sky, and is lit by LEDS, which are digitally programmed to mutate from warm oranges through to icy blues. This glamorous eyrie offers barflies an eagle's eye view of the metropolis.

LEFT
Bright oranges and pinks immediately single Praq out as a fun and casual venue.

ABOVE
One special orange table is moulded into the shape of a car.

ABOVE RIGHT
Another table appears to be supported by stacked plates and bowls.

When asked to create a child-friendly restaurant, Frank Tjepkema and Janneke Hooymans – the duo behind Amsterdam-based design agency Tjep. – seized the opportunity with gusto, not least because they were new parents themselves. 'One of the things we got annoyed about was when you take your small kid to restaurants people look at you in desperate ways, especially in Holland,' explains Tjepkema. 'Our client was Greek, and he said in southern Europe and Greece taking your children to restaurants is fine and people aren't annoyed by children. Loads of parents have this problem in Holland and don't want to go to McDonalds, so we tried to create an environment that's fresh and trendy for the parents but at the same time playful for the kids.'

At first, the local residents weren't so convinced of their concept. Restaurant Praq was to occupy a space in an affluent Dutch village that had been home to quite a traditional, conservative restaurant for 30 years. They even objected to the name, initially Prak, which in Dutch describes mashed up baby food. 'They changed the "k" to a "q" to take it away from the original word and make it

sound a bit more French and sophisticated, but for us it meant the logo turned out well, with a nice balance between the "p" and the "q",' explains Tjepkema.

The interior is typically Tjep., conceptual but also fun and colourful, with stylish decorative elements. Aside from the bright, primary palette, star attractions designed to appeal to kids include mobile waiter stations redolent of wheelbarrows, an orange table for four, shaped like a car, and an orange glass table balancing on legs that resemble cups, plates and bowls stacked on top of each other.

Interactive features likely to keep children entertained for longer include a long 'drawing' table supporting a rail to which is attached a giant roll of white paper and numerous pens and pencils for a spot of communal creativity. There is also a wall installation that resembles Meccano. Explains Tjepkema: 'It's a big puzzle that also refers to the typography of the restaurant logo, which is based on a potato masher utensil, so people can interact with the whole identity of the restaurant.'

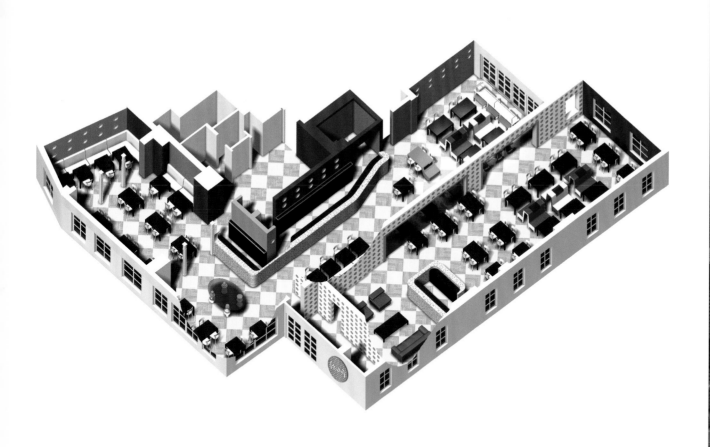

Always keen to contextualize their interior in its location, Tjep. decorated the long bar with a pretty blue floral pattern. 'It covers the entire bar without any breaks or interruptions, it was designed to work three-dimensionally on the computer. It's an old Dutch pattern. We try to include something that is relevant to the area.' The former restaurant also makes an appearance in the unique wall lighting composed of second-hand plates. 'We collected the plates from markets and friends and then had a company drill a hole through the middle with water-jets so we could use them as light fittings. One of the plates is from the old restaurant.'

In spite of the residents' early objections, Praq has proved to be immensely popular and Tjep. is already looking at creating two more in suburbs or villages elsewhere in the Netherlands sometime in 2007. Watch out McDonalds.

ABOVE
Three-dimensional
computer model
of the 120-cover
restaurant. The orange
'car' table can be seen
right of centre, and the
drawing table is on the
top right.

RIGHT
Interactive elements
include a long
communal drawing table
for children.

NOBU BERKELEY ST

LONDON UK DAVID COLLINS STUDIO

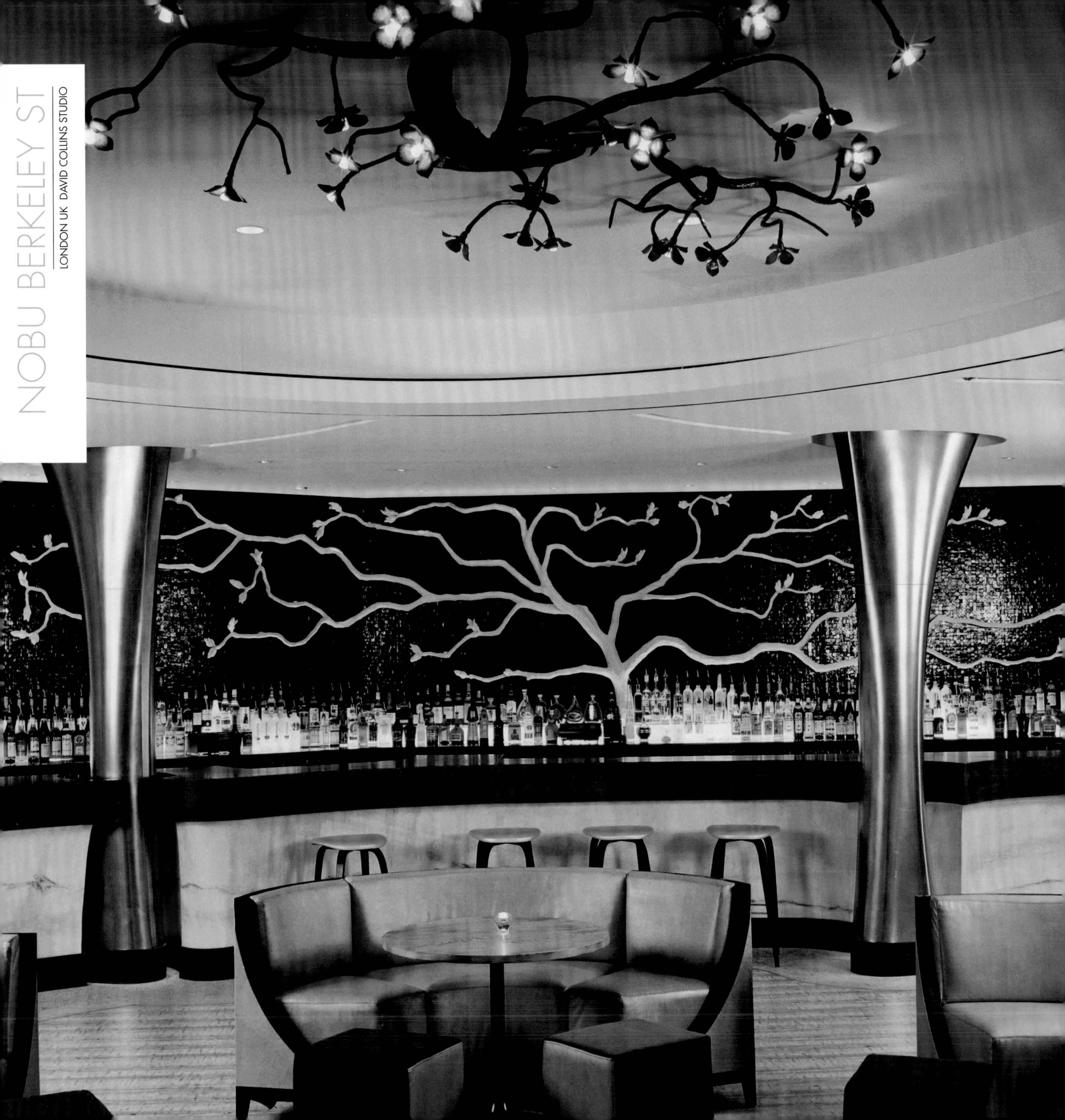

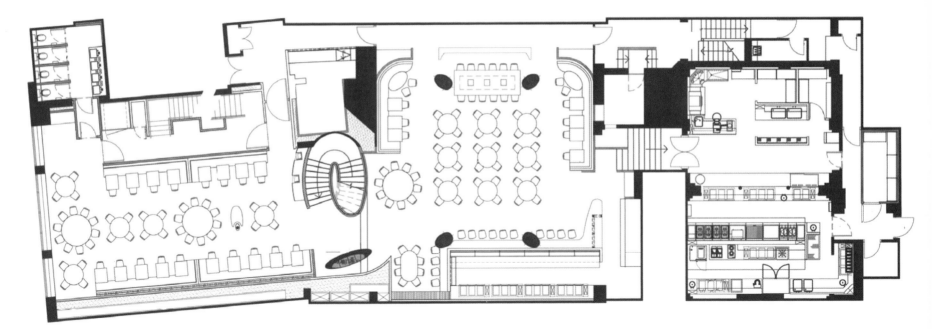

International chef Nobuyuki Matsuhisa now has eponymous restaurants serving his Japanese-Peruvian food in no less than 11 locations across the globe, from Malibu to Hong Kong. There are three in Manhattan and, since the opening of Nobu Berkeley St in August 2005, London can match this number. Who else to design the latest outpost but David Collins? The experienced Irish-born, London-based designer is the talent behind many of the capital's finest restaurant interiors, including The Wolseley and the Michelin-starred Locanda Locatelli and Pétrus to name a few.

Collins says: 'I didn't want Nobu Berkeley St to be themed in an "ethnic" sense, but rather that the flow of the architecture should influence the organic materials and shapes.' Transformation of the site, which previously housed the Mayfair Club, took four months, with the entire project taking 15 months in total. By employing flowing lines and organic forms inspired by trees, David Collins Studio has managed to create a seamless flow between the bar and restaurant levels, creating a cohesive sense of space and, as Collins says, keeping the customer connected to the energy of the interior.

As with many of its projects, David Collins Studio worked closely with craftspeople and artists to create bespoke details. Guests enter a light, winding reception lobby decorated by a mural by Malcolm Hill depicting a forest. This artwork features forms and a palette reminiscent of the paintings of Gustav Klimt, evoking a hint of fin-de-siècle decadence. This sensory amuse-bouche blossoms fully in the circular, ground-floor bar. Here, refined elements such as the curvaceous titanium-clad pillars, burnished walls of gold

graduating to silver, an arrangement of amoeba-like mini-mirrors and the pièce de résistance – the tree sculpture-cum-lighting – reinforce what appears to be a twenty-first-century interpretation of a Viennese Art Nouveau aesthetic.

The upper-level restaurant is accessed via a dramatic winding staircase clad in golden sheet metal combined with black Venetian plaster. There are two dining areas, situated on the right and left of the stairs. A cohesive look is maintained between the bar and the upstairs restaurant through a consistent use of materials, colour palette and artworks, including silver birch flooring, metallic columns and pistachio-green leather-upholstered banquettes paired with simple, light oak tables. 'I spotted the silver birch floor

ABOVE
A semi-abstract
tapestry of organic
ferns decorates one
wall of the lower-
level dining area.

RIGHT
The decadent,
ground-floor lounge
bar with its
burnished metallic
walls.

in a furniture shop in Sitges,' says Collins. 'It's inexpensive and environmentally friendly but did cause issues with the acoustics which we had to solve, but we learn from these experiences.'

Turning left at the top of the stairs, guests step up to a slightly more authentically Japanese dining area with an open kitchen. Its walls are clad in fumed and limed oak, and there is a traditional Hibachi table where diners can witness the chefs in action. Sake bottles provide decoration, with individual bottles housed in illuminated circular apertures cut into the timber and arranged in colourful concentric formations.

Running across one wall in the lower-level dining area is a 10 metre- (33 foot-) long abstract tapestry of vertical green forms resembling trees, or waving grasses. Composed of velvet applied to a shimmering background of white mesh backed with gold, this artwork lends a textured and handcrafted element to the scheme. 'This was more or less created in my studio with me choosing the colours,' explains Collins. 'I loved making the maquette; it was a very "hands on" experience.' His sentiment is very much in keeping with the delicate, carefully sculpted food created by Nobu's chefs which, together with the glamorous environment, has so far ensured that Nobu Berkeley St is possibly the most desirable restaurant in town.

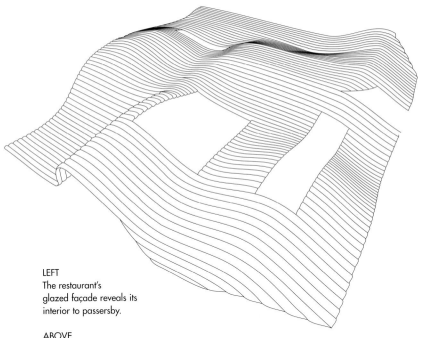

LEFT
The restaurant's glazed façade reveals its interior to passersby.

ABOVE
Computer rendering of the undulating slatted ceiling.

BELOW
Plan of the restaurant, which seats 228 diners (centre) and 23 guests at the bar (bottom).

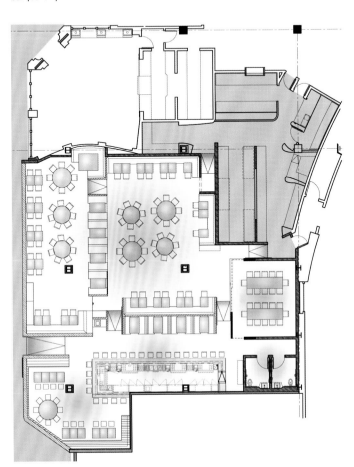

Graft's success has been swift. The progressive Los Angeles- and Berlin-based firm was formed in 1998 and is run by the trio of Lars Krückeberg, Wolfram Putz and Thomas Willmeit. Not just famous for being Brad Pitt's architects of choice, in 2004 they received critical acclaim for the interiors of the Q! Hotel in Berlin. Here, seeking to challenge the 'museum typology' of hotel interiors, the team morphed and blurred walls into floors and ceilings into walls, creating a futuristic internal landscape likened by some to a post-modern skate park. A slew of commissions followed, including several in America's current culinary and design hotspot, Las Vegas.

It was the Hollywood connection that secured Graft the commission to design Fix. Entrepreneur Andrew Sassoon of the Light Group – operators of the Caramel lounge and Light nightclub in the Bellagio Hotel & Casino – heard about Graft's work for Pitt, engineered a meeting and then hired them to create a hip, informal restaurant in the Bellagio. Their interior was completed in June 2004 and is as structurally dramatic as the Q! Hotel, with one grand gesture shaping the 372 square metre (4,000 square foot) space. Instead of blurring vertical and horizontal boundaries, Graft has radically landscaped the ceiling to resemble the underside of a sandy cave smoothly eroded by waves, or earthy red desert dunes turned upside down.

The structure is composed of 113 slats of Costa Rican padouk wood, each uniquely shaped and suspended from steel wire of varying lengths to create the contours. 'As a complex and supernaturally glowing topography, the ceiling plane acts as a façade for Fix and guides visitors into the space,' explain Graft. 'The slats alternately converge into smooth surfaces and diverge to create openness and translucency.' Within the swooping timber curves are concealed all the service elements, such as speakers, sprinklers, air-conditioning and the orange-gelled lights that set the interior warmly aglow.

Graft has also used padouk wood for the tables, booths and chairs, reinforcing the holistic nature of the space. Simple, cream faux-leather upholstery maintains a casual-dining feel. A low wall of padouk wood, echoing the curves of the ceiling, surrounds the restaurant, separating it from the gaudiness of slot machines and the general casino floor.

LEFT
Semiramis is a
complete Rashid
rainbow production
right down to the
placemats and
ashtrays.

RIGHT
Rashid's
'Bloob' stools,
manufactured by
Frighetto, line the
bar.

FAR RIGHT
Neon swirls light
the dining room
by night.

BELOW RIGHT
Ground-floor plan.
Hospitality areas
spill out onto the
terrace encircling
the biomorphic
pool (top left).

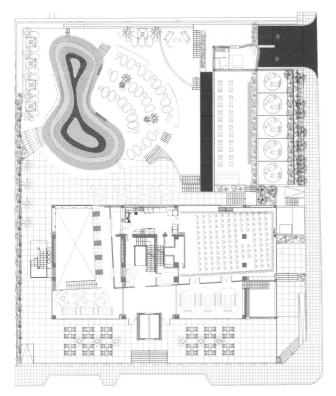

Entering the Semiramis Hotel is like floating into a 1960s acid trip, wild with candy colours and blobby forms. The 52-room boutique hotel opened in the affluent Athens suburb of Kifissia in May 2004 – strategically to coincide with the 2004 Athens Olympics – and is the technicolour vision of New York-based industrial designer Karim Rashid. Owner Dakis Joannou, a civil engineer, architect and avid contemporary art collector, commissioned Rashid to refurbish and change the façade of an existing hotel, for a budget of $25 million.

The result has been described as a 'hyper form of retro', and with its curvy pool, rainbow colours and bulbous forms, it seems to be daringly twenty-first-century while at the same time echoing a pastel-hued Miami, 1950s poolside California, the colourful cartoon world of the Jetsons and a feelgood, Pop Art sensibility. Although this is Rashid's first hotel, he is no stranger to the hospitality field, having previously designed Morimoto in Philadelphia (featured in *Restaurant Design*, 2004) and the ill-fated New York club Powder. Semiramis exhibits many of the layering techniques with coloured glass that Rashid used in the design of the latter. As he once said: 'In the material environment today there are so many new materials that can allow us to project the space infinitely; we take pieces of glass, films, all kinds of layering and light and are perpetually trying to find a way to create immaterial space.'

The restaurant and lounge bar occupy two floors; at lobby level there is a restaurant seating 40 diners where breakfast is served. The main 120-seat restaurant, which serves modern Mediterranean food, occupies the lower poolside level. Connecting them is a double-height lounge, furnished with Rashid's white and black 'Spline' sofas and chairs, teamed with glossy lime-coloured glass tables. Hot pink 'Omni' sofas line the windows.

By night the lounge is lit by starry, colour-changing fibre-optics embedded in a bio-morphic 'belly' that protrudes from the ceiling. Orange laminated glass forms the balustrade around the lobby-level dining area. This extends down through the double-height space to become a slanting translucent wall between the lounge and bar area, with access between the two provided by amoeba-shaped cut-outs.

The neighbouring dining room overflows onto the poolside patio and is a complete Rashid production with the furniture, tableware, menus and napkins all custom-designed for Semiramis. The restaurant really comes alive at night when its neon backdrop of colour-changing lighting throws the diners into silhouette, casting reflections across the pool outside.

LEFT
The Rococo ceiling painting was revealed in the course of the refurbishment.

ABOVE
The narrower end of the dining salon. The high-gloss black walls and rows of bulbs lend the space a distinctly nighttime feel.

ABOVE RIGHT
Betak designed all the furniture, which was custom-made by Domeau & Pérès in Paris.

How fitting that a venue in Paris's exclusive 8th arrondissement, which was once the haunt of French rock stars during the 1960s and 1970s, should today be resurrected by a modern day rock star. Former lead singer of seminal Seattle grunge band Soundgarden and current lead singer of Audioslave, Chris Cornell describes his fashionable new hangout as 'a restaurant-slash-bar where you're gonna hear rock music', (seattlepi.com, 21 April 2006). Cornell who, prior to his music career, worked for years as a chef at a seafood restaurant back home in Seattle, is now based in Paris. He teamed up with his brother-in-law Nick Blast, artistic director of The Plaza Athénée and a DJ, and nightclub owner Addy Bakhtiar, to create BC.

The proposed name of the new venue, BC, was initially an acronym of Blast and Cornell's surnames, but then they discovered the restaurant's colourful past as La Calavados. Serge Gainsbourg immortalized the nightspot in his song 'Rendez-vous à la Calavados' and

over the years, as a club and then restaurant, it has hosted the likes of Josephine Baker, Orson Welles, Jackie Onassis and Eartha Kitt. BC now stands for Black Calavados because of the overwhelmingly black interior dreamt up by Alexandre de Betak, the artistic director responsible for the shows of Dior, Hussein Chayalan and Viktor & Rolf among others. Betak says: 'black is a favourite blank canvas for me, a good starting point from which to create a warm and intimate environment and only highlight what I believe should be.'

BC consists of two floors: an intimate 44-seat upper-level restaurant serving 'New American' food, and a lower-level bar. Little could be altered structurally due to the historic nature of the late-nineteenth-century property, however Betak, who was allowed free rein, has given the interior a strong twenty-first-century noir look. 'One of the big challenges was to keep humility in the approach to the space,' Betak explains. 'To respect it and its vibe, because it's an old, beautiful building that has a certain

type of history that I wanted to preserve, but modernize' (fashionweekdaily.com, 8 March 2006).

In the dining room, black lacquered floors, high-gloss walls of black resin, smoked mirrors and custom-designed black furniture are lit by a single row of oversized clear light bulbs lining the upper walls – reminiscent of backstage dressing-room vanity lighting and flattering to all. The only colour present is above diners' heads; during the course of the renovation a stunning mythological-themed Rococo ceiling painting dating from around 1780 was discovered. Now revealed in all its glory, the surrounding black accentuates the fresco's rich hues.

Below the restaurant is the bar, a slender space with walls lined in reflective satin stainless-steel and black alcantara banquettes. Brilliant candlelight-coloured neon lighting, affixed to the walls or contained within glass cube-shaped tables, provides drama and contrast. The

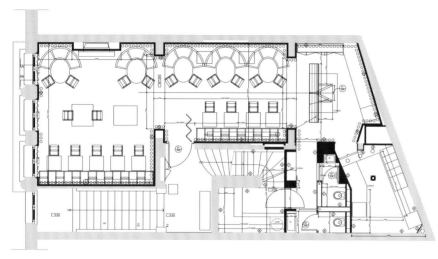

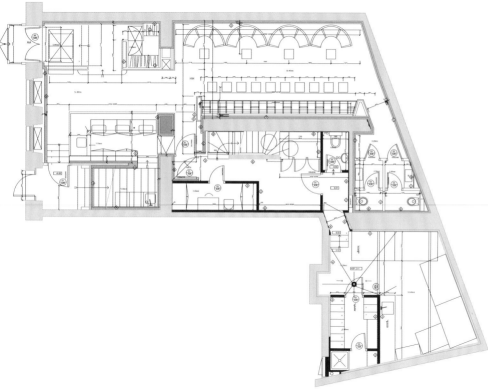

LEFT
Upper- and lower-level plans. Black Calavados comprises two interconnecting dining rooms on the upper floor with a bar below.

RIGHT
The lower-level bar is dramatically lit by candlelight-coloured neon along the walls and in the little cube tables.

effect has been aptly described as 'what it might be like to sip Bellinis inside a Xerox machine' (Blender.com, October 2006).

Betak's little black boîte opened during fashion week in March 2006 and has proved as indispensable to the Paris fashion crowd as the chic shade of black itself. Dubbed a 'hautespot', it has even inspired a catwalk show: 'I discovered a metal I loved, and I showed it to John Galliano and we used it for the January couture show,' said Betak (fashionweekdaily.com, 8 March 2006). It's clearly the new black.

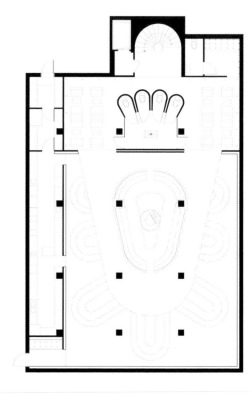

Since clubbing has lost its edge and consumers have become increasingly restaurant and food savvy, venues that blur the boundaries between restaurant, cocktail bar and club have grown in popularity. Often referred to as 'supperclubs', these places morph from restaurant into lounge club as the night wears on. Peacock Dinner Club claims to be the first of its kind in Sweden. Located in the centre on Gothenburg's lively restaurant and bar strip Kungsportsavenyn (known locally as 'the Avenue' and comparable to Barcelona's La Rambla), the Peacock was designed by young architect duo Andreas Lyckefors and John Olsson and opened in March 2006.

Inspiration for the design came from the venue's former incarnation – although recently the basement had lain empty, during the 1960s it was a well-frequented nocturnal hangout known as the Blue Peacock. It was these halcyon years that the new owners, a group of young bartenders-turned-entrepreneurs, wanted to recapture. In response to their clients' brief, which was to create a 'fancy restaurant that slowly evolves into a pumping house club in the early hours', OlssonLyckefors

based their concept, from the layout to the colour palette and finishes, on the iridescent fan shape of a peacock's tail feathers.

All original fittings were removed, except for essential support columns. At the heart of the new interior is an island bar (also containing the DJ booth), clad in reflective gold laminate. Surrounding this are seating booths in a fan-like configuration, integrated into an elevated horseshoe-shaped platform. Diaphanous black drapes between booths provide an element of intimacy for diners, however these are drawn back as the evening progresses and partying takes over. Upholstered in black leather, the booths are designed with durability and multi-purpose usage in mind: 'They allow eating during restaurant hours, sitting on the backs from both sides as the music volume increases and, finally, they function as podiums for dancing later on,' explains Lyckefors.

Just like a peacock's tail, lustre, radiance and colour provide the eye-catching glamour in this subterranean

space. Illuminated walls, which comprise perforated MDF backlit by RGB lights, twinkle with a feather-like motif by graphic designer Niklas Hultman. 'The colours work with the music in setting the mood,' says Lyckefors. 'We use soft light in calm colours in the early evening and it intensifies to pulsating bright colours later on.'

Adorning the dividing wall between the restaurant-club space and the entrance lobby, and adding to the overall shimmer and glow of the interior, is a sparkling panel of 14,000 golden sequins arranged in the image of a peacock's tail. Even the toilet design has been influenced by the peacock theme. OlssonLyckefors cast four towering, industrial-style cubicles in green-tinted concrete: 'spread out like the peacock's tail they each stand alone, allowing guests arriving in the bar to catch glimpses through into the shared washroom space.' Thanks to OlssonLyckefors it seems this peacock is reborn and proudly strutting its stuff once again.

PREVIOUS PAGES

Illuminated walls
change colour to alter
the mood over the
course of the evening.

THIS PAGE

FAR LEFT
Booths accommodate
70 diners and later on
function as podia for
dancing.

LEFT
Plan. The seating
arrangements and even
the toilets (top) follow
the shape of a
peackock's tail feathers.

RIGHT
The bar stools are
deigned by Konstantin
Grcic.

CREDITS AND INDEX

PROJECT CREDITS

AROLA
www.arola-madrid.com
Architect: Ateliers Jean Nouvel
www.jeannouvel.fr
Local Architect: Alberto Medem et B720
Interiors: Vidal y Asociados Arquitectos
www.lvidal.com
Client: Museo Nacional Centro de Arte
Reina Sofía (MNCARS)
Ministerio de Cultura
Engineers: Esteyco and J.G. Asociados
Consultants: Higini Arau and Rafael Guijarro
Project Architect: Alberto Medem
Assistant Architects: David Fagard, Gian-Luca
Ferrarini, Jérémie Lebarillec, Sergio Noero,
Florence Rabiet, Sophie Thullier, Mounie El
Hawat, Gian-Luca Ferrarini, Anne Lamiable,
Agustin Miranda, Carlos Nogueira, Adelino
Magalhaes, Eloisa Siles, Marcos Velasco,
Fermina Garrido, Antonia García, Rafael
Cañizares, Barbara Belloso, Higinio Esteban,
Javier Piedra, Raul Pleite, Camila Campo
Quantity Surveyor: Rafael Guijarro
Model: Jean-Louis Courtois
Perspective: Didier Ghislain
Computer renderings: Artefactory

BG RESTAURANT
Architect/Interior Designer: Kelly Wearstler,
Interior Design (kwid)
www.kwid.com
Client: Bergdorf Goodman / Neiman Marcus
Structural and Mechanical Engineer: Sweet
Construction Corp.

BISTRO & EL MERCADO
www.faenahotelanduniverse.com
Design: Philippe Starck
www.philippe-starck.com

BLACK BOX AÏZONE
Architect / Interior Designer: Bernard Khoury
www.bernardkhoury.com
Design team: DW5, Bernard Khoury, Patrick
Mezher and Yasmine el Machnouk
Engineer: Home Works

BLACK CALAVADOS
www.blackcalavados.com
Design: Alexandre de Betak, Bureau Betak
www.bureaubetak.com
Funiture upholstery: Domeau & Peres
Furniture metalwork: msi
Lounge neons: Feerick

BLITS
www.blits-rotterdam.nl
Interior Design: Marcel Wanders Studio
www.marcelwanders.com
Architect: Francine Houben
Client: Hotel New York Group

BON
Design: Philippe Starck
www.philippe-starck.com

BUDDAKAN
www.buddakannyc.com
Interior designer: Christian Liaigre
www.christian-liaigre.fr
Coordination: Goto Design Group
Lighting: Isometrix

BUDDHA-BAR
www.buddhabarnyc.com
Architecture & Interior Design: Dupoux Design
www.dupouxdesign.com
Interior Design Project Team: Stephane Dupoux,
Designer; Adi Sagie, Studio Director & Project
Manager; Walter Zamora, Creative Director
Contractor: Carlo Seneca, C & A Seneca
Construction LLC
Consultants:
Skylight Design: Didi Pei,
Pei Partnership Architects LLP
Lighting: Robert Singer,
Robert Singer & Associates, Inc.
Engineering: Alan R. Schwartz P.E.
Consulting and Angelos Georgopoulos P.E.
Consulting Engineer
Kitchen: Barplex
Expediter: RIP Construction Consultants, Inc.
Sound systems: Joe Lodi, Advanced Audio
Technologies
Architectural and decorative lighting provided
by: TBD (Technology By Design)
Custom designed furniture manufactured by:
d-mand (www.d-mand.com)

CANTEEN
Architects: Universal Design Studio
www.universaldesignstudio.com
M & E Engineers: Alan Guy Associates
Lighting Consultant: Wayne Parker
Structural Engineers: Price and Myers
Floor covering: Cork / HD88 Cork / Siesta
Cork Tile Company
Pendant lights: designed by Universal Design
Studio and produced by PPR
Central tables and benches: designed by
BarberOsgerby, manufactured by Isokon Plus
Textiles: Booth seating fabric supplied by Bute
Fabrics

CHÂTEAU RESTAURANT JOËL ROBUCHON
Interior Design: Glamorous Co., Ltd.
www.glamorous .co.jp
Lighting Consultant: Kenji Ito (Maxray, Inc.)
Contractor: Tanseisha Co., Ltd.
In-house project team: Yasumichi Morita,
Takuma Sato
Client: Four Seeds Corporation
Furniture: Complex (Lef Inc.)
Curtain & Carpet: National Trading, Inc.
Swarovski: Daigo Boeki Co., Inc.

COPPER BLEU
www.copperbleu.com
Designers: Jordan Mozer + Associates Limited
www.mozer.com
Design Team: Jordan Mozer, Principal;
Jeff Carloss, Architect ; Beverlee Mozer,
Product Manager; Siamak Mostoufi, Designer;
Matt Winter, Product Design; Brad Schenkel,
Designer; Tim Schwarz, Designer
Architect of Record / Local Team: Cuningham
Group Architecture, P.A.; John W. Cuningham,
Principal; David M. Solner, Principal; Ryan
Lovelle, Project Manager; Adam Wilbrecht;
Jim Grzybowski
Structural Engineer: Lindau Companies, Inc.;
Bill Lindau, P.E.
General Contractor: Kraus-Anderson
Construction Co.; Jon Boerboon, Project
Manager; Dave Carlson, Site Superintendent
Management Team: Restaurant Tour, LLC; Scott
Winer, Restaurant Developer; Deborah
Jacobson, Director of Operations; Jim Jacobson
Hempel Properties: Jon Hempel, Project
Manager; Tobie Nidetz Consulting;
Tobie Nidetz, Consulting Chef

COSPAIA
www.cospaia.be
Interior Design general: Marcel Wolterinck
www.wolterinck.com
Project partners at Wolterinck: Nancy Torreele
(Interior Designer) and Nicole Schinkelshoek
(Interior Architect)
Client: Mr. Jan Tindemans
Installations: Verbruggen Contractor Belgium,
Pierre van den Broeck
Construction Belgium
Furniture: Designs Wolterinck
Furniture retail: Meridiani, Enrico Pellizoni,
Marie's Corner, Makomin,
Mary and Virvaire
Fabrics: Home collection Wolterinck
and Elitis France
Wall covering: Limited Edition belgium,
pictures Philippe Bourseiller
Garden design: Marcel Wolterinck

LE CRISTAL ROOM
Design: Philippe Starck
www.philippe-starck.com
Client: Baccarat

DAR EL YACOUT
Design: Studio Carratta
Owner: Medina S.r.l.
Construction: Grandi Appalti S.r.l.
Iron and metal: M.C.M. S.r.l.
Artistic glass: Luberto Piero
Artistic stones: Zezza Nicola
Water falls: Cascade
Reconstituted marble: Lucchi S.r.l.
Gold texture: Bisazza S.r.l.
Moroccan zelij, furniture and accessories:
La Maison Bleue – Marrakech

EVO
Architects: Richard Rogers Partnership
and Alonso i Balaguer Arquitectes
www.richardrogers.co.uk
Interior Design: GCA Arquitectes Associats
www.gcaarq.com

FABBRICA
www.fabbrica.nl
Design: Tjep.
www.tjep.com

FASANO
www.fasano.com.br
Architecture: Isay Weinfeld
www.isayweinfeld.com
Collaborator: Domingos Pascali
Project Managaer: Elena Scarabotolo
Team: Sophia Lin, Fabio Rudnik, Flavia Oide,
Carolina Maluhy, Priscila Araujo
General Contractor: Racional Engenharia
Structural Consultant: Aluizio A. M.
D'ávila Associados
Mechanical, Electrical And Plumbing
Engineering: Mha Engenharia
Air Conditioning Engineering: Ambient Air
Acoustic Consultant: Akkermann
Projetos Acústicos
Cooking Facilities Consultant: Estillo Arquitetura
Landscaping Designing: Isabel Duprat
Paisagismo

FIN
www.mirage.com
Interior Design Firm: Yabu Pushelberg
Owner: MGM Mirage
Art: James Robertson Art Consultants
Hanging sculpture in the back of restaurant:
Artist – Hirotoshi Sawada
Floating resin spheres in the main dining room:
Artist – Helen Poon
Silver horse: James Robertson Art Consultants
Pollack fabric on dining chairs and banquette
seating: Primavera Interior Furnishings Ltd.
Banquette back fabric: Rudolph Inc.
Yabu Pushelberg-designed carpet:
The Sullivan Source
Hanging glass spheres, silk screen
with mountain motif & glass crystal
cubes on glass wall: D'art
Dining chairs: Kline
Handmade tiles: Pascale Girardin

FIX
Design: GRAFT
www.graftlab.com
Client: LIGHT LV, Andrew Sasson
GRAFT Project Team: Lars Krückeberg,
Wolfram Putz, Thomas Willemeit, Dana Bauer,
Narineh Mirzaeian, Helena Otzen

FRISSON
www.frissonsf.com
Interior Design, Concept Consultation, Lighting

Design: Scott Kester, Kester Inc
www.scottkester.com
Architect of Record: Architecture TM,
Tim Murphy, John Seamon
Project Management: Hasz Construction,
Karl Hasz
General Contractor: Terranova Industries,
Ron Taylor
Kitchen Design: MSNRCD,
Mark Stech-Novak
Garden Design: Paxton Gate, Sean Quigly
Graphic Design: Louise Fili Ltd, Louise Fili
Structural Engineering: ZFA Engineering,
Ahmad Issa
Mechanical Electrical Engineering:
Acies Engineering
Acoustical Engineering: Charles Salter
Associates
Art Installation: Catherine Wagner
Dome Fabrication: Boyett Construction
Screen Fabrication: Eclipse Design
Millwork Fabrication: Glacier DRS Inc,
Dave Renfrow
Audio: JK Sound
3-D Modelling: Neurolapse, Harold Gainer

GILT
www.giltnewyork.com
Concept & Interior Design: Patrick Jouin
www.patrickjouin.com
Project Team: Sanjit Manku (Director), Marie
Deroudilhe (Project Manager), Karri Campbell,
Ramy Fischler
Owner: New York Palace Hotel
Lighting Design: James Long Lighting
Graphic Design: Philippe David, Paris
Architect of Record: Augustine M. Digneo
Millwork Contractor: Mueller Custom Cabinetry
Dining room chairs & armchairs (Patrick
Jouin design): Laval
Bar club chairs (Patrick Jouin design): Deltag
Custom bronze and caramel leathers: Edelman
Custom stainless steel back-bar:
Infinity Stainless Products
Custom mirrored glass pebbles on side of
entrance stair: Elements Glass
Madison Room custom carpet: Carpet Diem
Existing gilded mouldings restoration: Mustiga
Refinishing & Restoration

INN THE PARK
www.innthepark.com
Architect: Hopkins Architects Ltd.
www.hopkins.co.uk
Sir Michael Hopkins
Andrew Barnett (Director)
Gary Clark (Project Director)
Margaret Leong (Project Architect)
Stephen Jones (Architect)
Arifa Salim (Administrator)
Client: William Weston, Chief Executive,
The Royal Parks Agency
Project Manager: Bucknall Austin Limited
Engineers: ARUP

Quantity Surveyor: Bucknall Austin Limited
Restaurateur: Gruppo
Interior Fittings: Tom Dixon
Main Contractor: Ashe Construction Ltd
Piling: Roger Bullivant Ltd
Concrete: John Cooper Construction Ltd
Joinery: Swift Horseman Ltd
Green roof: Erisco Bauder
Architectural metalwork: Mercantile met tech ltd
M&E Services: E&B Engineering Services Group

ISOLA BAR & GRILL
www.isolabarandgrill.com
Design: Leigh & Orange
www.leighorange.com.hk
Design Team: Hugh Zimmern, Ricky Hung,
Phyllis Doo, Terry Chu, Iris Cheung, Randy Agus
Client: Gaia Group
Consultants: Far East Consulting Engineers,
C.E.C. Catering Equipment Co Ltd, Light
Directions Ltd, Hanson Associates,
Lilian Tang Design
Main Contractor: Ocean Contracting Ltd.

LÁGRIMAS NEGRAS
www.hotelpuertamerica.com
Design: Christian Liaigre
www.christian-liaigre.fr

LEVER HOUSE RESTAURANT
www.leverhouse.com
Interior design: Marc Newson
with associated architect Sébastien Segers
www.marc-newson.com
www.sebastiensegers.com
Client: RFR Realty – Joshua Pickard, John
McDonald, Robert Nagle, Aby Rosen
Architect of record: CAN resources –
Taavo Somer, Derek Sanders, Judy Wong
Associate architect: MGA Architecture –
Walter Radtke
Lighting Design: L'Observatoire International –
Herve Descottes
General contractor: Tri-Star Construction Corp.
MEP Engineer: Vogel Taylor Engineers LLP
Structural Engineer: SuperStructures
Custom furniture: Meritalia

THE LINE
Project Team:
Principal: Adam D. Tihany, Tihany Design
Senior Project Designer: Rafael Alvarez
Senior Designer and Project Manager:
Carolyn Ament
Interior Designer: Peter K. Lu
www.tihanydesign.com
Client: Shangri-la Hotel, Singapore
Architect of Record: Chao Tse Ann
& Partners PTE LTD
Food Service Consultant: Creative Kitchen
Planners Asia Pacific
Structural Engineer: Buro Engineering PTE LTD
MEP Engineer: Buro Engineering PTE LTD
Electrical Engineer: Alpha

Audio/Visual: Alpha
Signage Consultant: Corlette Design
Quantity Surveyor: KPK Quantity Surveyors
PTE LTD General Contractor: Park International
Interior PTE LTD
Kitchen Supplier: Fabristeel Private Limited
Solid orange light boxes:
Consort Contractors PTE LTD
Striped orange light boxes:
Park International Interior PTE LTD
Custom-made art films: Bram Tihany

THE MANSION
www.the-mansion.nl
Designer: Concrete Architectural Associates
www.concreteamsterdam.nl
Client: Andy Martin
Project team: Rob Wagemans, Joris Angevaare,
Erik van Dillen
Project Architect: Joris Angevaare
Furniture: Horstermeer Bouw en Interieur bv
Light and sound: Vasco Show Techniek
Electrical and plumbing: Unica Installatie
techniek
Air conditioning: Silva Luchttechniek
Kitchen equipment: Horequip
Soft furnishings: Wave totaalinrichting
Wall covering and paint: Veerman Volendam
Drywall and ceilings: Kwakman Volendam
Floor: Bembé Parkett
Synthetic cornice: Proga Kunststoffen bv
Prints: Vertical Vision
Chandeliers: Seels & Sezamstraat
Consultants: E & E project management

MEGU MIDTOWN
www.megunyc.com
Interior Design: Glamorous Co., Ltd.
www.glamorous.co.jp
Lighting Consultant: Kenji Ito (Maxray, Inc.)
General contractor: Kudos Construction Corp.
In-house project team: Yasumichi Morita, Shingo
Abe, Aki Sakuramoto
Client: Food Scope America, Inc.
Furniture: Lcm Group, Lee Custom Millwork Inc.
Construction Supervisor: Toshihiko Hashimoto
(Toshi Enterprise, Inc.)
Photographer: Mitsuhiro Susa
Ukiyoe artist: Gaku Azuma

MIX
www.thehotelatmandalaybay.com
Interior Design: Patrick Jouin
www.patrickjouin.com
Interior Design Project Team: Patrick Jouin
& Director Sanjit Manku with
Marie Deroudilhe (Project Architect) and Claudia
Del Bubba (Senior Interior designer)
Architecture Firm: Klai Juba Architects
Project Architect: Robert White
Owner: Mandalay Development
Client rep.: 1027 Design Management
Sound Design: Savi
Custom Millwork: Mueller Custom Cabinetry

Lighting: L'Observatoire International
MEP Engineering: JBA Consulting Engineers
Structural Engineering: Lochsa Engineering
Graphics: Philippe David
General Contractor: Mandalay Development

THE MODERN
www.themodernnyc.com
Architect/Interior Designer: Bentel & Bentel,
Architects/Planners LLP
www.bentelandbentel.com
Design Team (B&B): Paul Bentel, FAIA,
Peter Bentel AIA, Carol Rusche Bentel, FAIA,
Susan Nagle ASID, Raffaele Razzano,
Thomas O'Connor, Chris Hinchey, Peter Halkias,
Ben Cruz, Rob Costello
Client: The Museum of Modern Art (MoMA)
Restaurateur: Union Square Hospitality Group
Lighting Designer: George Sexton Associates
Structural Engineer: Severud Associates
Mechanical Engineer: GC Eng and Associates

MOO
www.hotelomm.es
Interior Designer: Sandra Tarruella
& Isabel López
Architect: Juli Capella

NOBU BERKELEY ST
Design: David Collins Studio
www.davidcollins.com
Client: Como Holdings

PATINA
Design: Belzberg Architects, Hagy Belzberg,
AIA, principal
www.belzbergarchitects.com
Project Team: Eric Stimmel, Manish Desai,
Erik Sollom, Ryan Thomas, Melanie Freeland,
Dan Rentsch
Consultants: John Dorius & Associates
(mechanical), A+F Consulting Engineers
(electrical), Daniel Echeto (structural, restaurant),
John A. Martin Associates (structural, building),
Tom Nasrollahi & Associates (plumbing),
Martin Newson Associates (acoustic),
Ernie Cancio (kitchen), Elizabeth Paige Smith
(colours & materials), Spectrum Oak (millwork)
Contractor: Matt Construction
Construction Manager: David Schwanke

PEACOCK DINNER CLUB
www.peacockdinnerclub.com
Architect/Interior Designer: OlssonLyckefors
Architects
www.olssonlyckefors.se
Design Team: Andreas Lyckefors, Johan Olsson,
Frida Sjöstam
Client: Stefan Stömberg, Jens Odén,
Johan Däldehög, Henrik Carlsson
Technical light consultant: Cardi
Structural Engineer: Convesta, Aröds inredningar

RAMA
Design: Jeffrey Beers International
www.jeffreybeers.com

RESTAURANT BAR CLUB 11
www.ilove11.nl
Concept and Design: Studio's Müller en Van Tol
– Bas Van Tol and Floris Kindt
www.mullervantol.nl
Technical advisor: Ontwerpers A'dam –
Erik Hehenkamp
Executor 'up and over' panels: Frank Hoogveld
Upholsterer: Linkk basics – Jacko Mensink
Upholstery: Vescom
Chairs: Moroso

RESTAURANT PRAQ
www.praq.nl
Design: Tjep.
www.tjep.com

SEMIRAMIS RESTAURANT
www.semiramishotels.gr
Designer: Karim Rashid Design
www.karimrashid.com
Design team: Karim Rashid, Camila Tariki,
Jalan Sahba
Client: Dakis Joannou
Architect of Record: K. Kyriakidis & Associates
Lighting Consultant: Focus Lighting
Furniture and lighting: designed by Karim Rashid
for Frighetto, Magis, Nienkamper, Zeritalia,
Fasem, Kovacs, Foscarini, Zerodesigno, Idee,
Edra, Galerkin, Pure Design
Floor: Bisazza terrazzo slabs,
Brintons custom carpets
Wall: Coloured glass, Wolf Gordon Wallpaper

SENDERENS
www.senderens.fr
Design: Noé Duchaufour Lawrance
Executive architect: Axel Schoenert,
ASAA Company

SEOUL SOUL
Design: Zokei-Syudan Co., Ltd.
www.zokei-syudan.co.jp
Client: Gendai-Kikaku, Inc.

SHIBUYA
Interior Design Firm: Yabu Pushelberg
Art: James Robertson Art Consultant
Japanese paper mâché sculpture:
Artist – Francesca Carllo
Custom banquette screens
and semi-private dining circular screens:
Artist – Hirotoshi Sawada
Wood block lantern sculptures: Artist – Umomo
Sap wood wall screens and darkened steel floor
inlay with laser-etched pattern (semi-private
dining): Dennis Lin and Lolah, Inc.
Acrylic wall feature: Marc Littlejohn, Inc. –
Acrylic Fabricating Services
Custom abstract wood dining table:

John Housmand
Table bases: Isa International, Inc.
Fabric for custom dining chair:
Primavera Interior Furnishings Ltd.
Edelman leather for custom dining chair:
Telio & Cie
Fabric for custom dining banquette: Maharam
Tempered clear glass with custom-etched vertical
pattern, laminated pink glass, tempered pink
colour glass with etched pattern on one side,
pink coloured mirror and frosted pink coloured
mirror: Sound Solutions
Custom chandelier and pendant light:
TPL Marketing
Ceramic tile flooring:
Stone Tile International, Inc.
Stone counter top (Sushi Counter):
Coverings Etc., Inc.
Stone counter top (Teppanyaki Counter):
Hiltz Marble and Granite
Clear frosted acrylic (Teppanyaki area)
and transparent pink acrylic (Saki Cellar):
Cyro Industries
Sushi Bar: The Sullivan Source

SIROCCO
Design: DWP
www.dwp.com
DWP Design team:
Scott Whittaker – Executive Sponsor
and Architect
Kristina Zanic – Interior Design Director
Khun Nongnut Bumrungkun – Architect
Khun Patipath Bunwanno – Architect
Khun Apisake Painupong
Client: Challenge Property Co. Ltd
Main contractor: Bovis Lend Lease
M&E: Meinhardt
Kitchen consultant: Romano Gatland
Furniture: Nadin
Flooring: Carpet International

SPICE MARKET
www.jean-georges.com
Design: Jacques Garcia

YAUATCHA
Design: Christian Liaigre
www.christian-liaigre.fr

AUTHOR'S ACKNOWLEDGEMENTS

Thanks to the team at Laurence King Publishing, in particular commissioning
editor Philip Cooper, editor Liz Faber, Fredrika Lökholm, Kim Sinclair and
Laura Willis. Lorraine Richer at Richer Design, I'm glad we finally managed
to collaborate – thank you for your clear vision and super efficiency. For
supplying the gorgeous plates introducing each chapter thanks to Pamela
Brice at Pedlars (pages 20–21), Sabine Leifert at Authentics (52–53),
Heal's, London (104–105) and Richard Scott at Purple (pages 144–145).

Ava Mae, thank you for being so fashionably, and fortuitously, late. May
you always eat well.

To the buyers of Restaurant Design (2004, Laurence King) thanks for making
the original version successful enough for a sequel. Long may your appetite
for fab restaurants and design books continue.

And finally, to the architecture and design practices, proprietors, press
officers, photographic agents and photographers who have spared their
time and provided me with the inspiration, information and material that has
made this book possible. This is book is dedicated to you all, keep 'em
coming…